Pricing Your Artwork with CONFIDENCE

An extensive step-by-step guide to pricing artwork and fine craftwork

© 2014, Alexandria Levin
Painted Jay Publishing, LLC
www.paintedjay.com

Updated and Revised

Pricing Your Artwork with CONFIDENCE

An extensive step-by-step guide to pricing artwork and fine craftwork

Published by Painted Jay Publishing, LLC
www.paintedjay.com

© 2014, Alexandria Levin
All Rights Reserved.
No part of this book may be reproduced or transmitted in any form or by any means whatsoever, electronic, mechanical or any other possible method, without permission in writing from the author, except for brief quotations in a book review.

ISBN: 978-0692261989
Second Edition, Updated and Revised
Published in the United States of America in 2014
Printed by CreateSpace

Cover painting: 'Trunk Bottom'
© 2009, Alexandria Levin

Acknowledgements

I am in gratitude to every experience I have ever had during my many years in the business end of being an artist. However any of them may have been perceived at the time, from positive to negative, each event added to the cumulative knowledge that became the source for this book.

I would also like to extend my deepest thanks to the broad network of artists and arts administrators (including many curators, galleries, collectors and other arts supporters) that I have been fortunate to know over the years. When we live in an extended community with a spirit of cooperation and communication, instead of competition and fear, amazing things can happen.

For Your Information / Disclaimer

This book was written for the purpose of offering friendly advice and encouragement. The author and publisher are not in the business of dispensing legal, accounting or any other licensed professional service. Always consult a legitimate accountant, attorney or other professional for assistance if needed.

The contents of this book are based on the author's own personal experiences and opinions, as well as on commonly held knowledge concerning the business of art. You are highly encouraged to read all available material on the subject, and to form your own business policies and personal opinions for yourself.

This book makes no promises concerning sales, marketing, career promotion or success by any definition. It was written only to impart knowledge. What you do with that knowledge is up to you. In order to succeed you must be willing to take complete responsibility for your own actions and decisions concerning your own level of success or financial well-being, by any definition.

Although this book has been written and edited to be as accurate as possible and to avoid any mistakes, there may be typographical or mathematical errors and/or omissions in content.

Any mention of any person, group or institution perceived to be negative is unintentional, is based purely on the author's own experience, is not reflective of anyone else's experience, and is included as an example only. Names have been omitted for this reason.

The author and Painted Jay Publishing LLC shall not be held liable or responsible to any person, group or entity in regards to any real, imagined or alleged loss or damage caused, either directly or indirectly, by anything written in or implied by this book.

This second edition is dedicated to the artists who reach out to help one another; with advice, a connection, shared opportunities, a spare tube of paint, or an empathetic ear.

Contents

Contents

Introduction

We are hunters and gatherers by nature.

We hunt at night, sometime gathering in groups, searching for inspiration at events and receptions. We gather ideas, we gather food, we gather connections. When opportunity makes an appearance, we go for the kill. Maybe a painting gets sold, an exhibition gets booked, or a better studio space is offered. We hunt because we have to. It's survival.

We hunt in the early mornings as dawn breaks over trash left on the curbside, because something really good is almost always hidden in that crumpled pile of refuse. Whatever it is, is in there, we know it. Our eyesight is sharp, our intuition is well-tuned. When our pockets are filled mostly with laundry lint, we have our best resource at hand. Our creativity. It is intelligence in motion.

Then why is it, with all our inherent brilliance, do we listen to the old myths and lies about how we cannot set a price to the physical manifestations of our imaginations? Why has the pricing of artwork been a mysterious issue for artists for as long as any of us can remember? Why is it not taught as a matter of course in art schools?

I suppose, money matters were for somebody else to think about, but certainly not for us artists. Maybe, we shouldn't have to worry our creative little heads about finances, pricing and the marketplace. The dealer, our prince charming, would rescue us from of those issues. If we were taught anything about the business end of being an artist, then it was about the basic promo packet; once-upon-a-time this was slides, now the CD of images, resume, statement, and the SASE. Maybe we would receive a bit of gallery protocol or slide lecture delivery, and not much else. And this was usually for the graduate level students. The undergraduates were often left to fend for themselves.

If money is so dirty, then why is that a problem when we are already covered in paint, charcoal, ink, sawdust and who knows what else?

Artists and Money

Money and art have a strange relationship. Because the art-making process can be so genuinely spiritual, money is often thought of as corrupting that which is sacred. If this is the case, then may I mention the noble professions of medicine, healing, ministry and teaching? People in these fields, and many more, expect to be paid for their labor, no matter how much love and care is packed into their work. Art dealers, museum staff, and other professionals in the arts; no one questions their need to be paid for their labors.

So, why should we have this problem?

If being an artist is a vocation, a calling, and if we work hard and put in the time, then we should be able to make a living. Not a scrounging or a foraging, but a decent living by doing what we do best. Considering that art is truly valuable to society, it would seem that the people who create art must be valued.

However, society seems to both adore and disdain artists at the same time. The starving artist myth is still alive and well. And if we are kept in the dark about the state of our financial affairs, then we can continue to feed this myth. Why is the starving artist still perpetuated as a stereotype? Here are a few possibilities:

1. Cheap art. Some people just want cheap art. If our expectations in life are lowered sufficiently, then maybe we will feel desperate enough to sell our work dirt cheap. Sell cheap or go hungry, they say. In this book you will see clearly that by selling your artwork cheap you will be more likely to starve, than otherwise.

2. Hobby. The fine arts are considered disposable, not really all that important to the day-to-day realities of life. The work we do is often diminished to hobby status, unless what we produce is functional, on a very slim definition of what functional means.

3. Envy. We have dared to live our dreams, while so many people haven't even tried. Some folks prefer that we fail or suffer in our attempts, so that they can feel okay about not taking the risk to chase their own dreams.

4. A sick romanticism. This is so that we can live out someone else's strange fantasies about how artists live.

Artists and Business

The relationship between art and business can be symbiotic, both mutually exclusive and beneficial. There is a difference between what you do in your studio and what you do in your office, even if they are on different sides of the same room. We are fortunate in that we can separate our creativity (and therefore our spirituality) from the marketplace. For artists, musicians, writers, choreographers and a few others, it's much easier to achieve this separation than it is for those in the spiritual, healing and nurturing professions. We can step away from the business side of things while we are doing our most important work.

What you do in your studio is one thing and what you do in your office space is another. If you're thinking about the marketplace while making your art, then you are letting the business side of things intrude where visual creativity needs to happen. But there is a clear difference between painting for the market and marketing your paintings. There is a market out there for anything (in any price range), therefore painting for a specific market can be detrimental to your vision, and is not really necessary. Most artists are too busy working at following their personal muses to be concerned with selling out. In my opinion, create what you will in your studio, what your heart, soul, spirit and mind tell you to create. Be a channel and be pure.

Outside the studio, when the piece is done or the day is over, then thoughts of the marketplace can enter. Business is a separate thing in another time frame in a different mode. It's easy to keep them apart. Sit at your desk or computer, pay the bills, send some email, prepare some digital images, look into exhibiting somewhere, follow up on a sale, check out a few other opportunities. It's really okay to sell your creations. They can support you in your endeavors. Selling your artwork is completely different than selling your soul.

Just Plain Money

Money is neither evil nor angelic. Having money doesn't make you a better person, more virtuous or divinely blessed. Neither is poverty a virtue, nor does suffering necessarily make one great. Having money, or not having it, is no reflection of your inherent worth as a human being. It's neutral. Money is just a tool, a form of barter, a common means of exchange. Water floods and drowns. Water nourishes crops and quenches thirst. Is water good or is water bad? With money, how you come by it, how you earn it and what you do with it is what matters.

Much human emotion is invested into the meaning of money. But money itself, both the mathematical numbers on a screen or a piece of paper and the physical stuff in your pocket or purse is emotionless. Having money makes some aspects of life easier to navigate, so having it is good, but it is neither good nor bad in and of itself. So, it is good to have money and not so good to not have it. Therefore, being an artist and desiring to have money exchanged for your artwork is definitely not a bad thing.

We are all born into different situations. In our lives, there are many "what ifs". As a child we have no control over these circumstances. Some people start with advantages that others don't have. Many aspects of the art world as it exists are unfair to artists who come from lesser means or who don't have financial support. Opportunities often seem to go towards those who have more money. It would be nice (to put it nicely) if this situation were different.

However, as much as this uneven playing field needs to be leveled somehow, it would be wrong to be judgmental of artists who have financial support. Assumptions of any kind should never be made about individuals, no matter what their circumstances. There are plenty of financially supported artists who are aware of and are grateful for what they have been given. They do their best by themselves and by others. At the same time, all the money in the world won't help you as an artist if you are told that you are no good at an early age, or if you are expected to simply let go of your dreams to please some tradition in the family.

Talent is born neither from money nor poverty. Persons born into affluence could choose their birth no more than those born into other circumstances. And a person should never be judged by what they were born, ever. Meanwhile, there are too many unfair disadvantages holding multitudes of truly talented artists back because of financial considerations, and the whole culture loses in the long run because of it.

I believe it is important to bring to light certain realities, those of which are clearly not judgments. Realizing that anything broken exists is the first step towards fixing it. So how do we level the playing field without destroying what is good? We don't want to take away from artists who have financial support and family connections. We want to add to those who don't have those things in order to make things fair. The ideal is to raise the level for everybody to have an equal opportunity for success based purely on talent, originality of vision and hard work. When that day comes, we will all benefit.

About this Book

This book is about the pricing of artwork. It is not about marketing, selling you as the artist, or how to sell your artwork. I have, however, come up with a clear formula for pricing artwork. I have read dozens of articles on pricing and dozens of art business books with chapters on pricing, and they were all quite vague in my opinion. The last thing I want to do is to supply more vague information. I have explored a number of diverse aspects of pricing quite thoroughly in this book, hopefully with clarity. Although this is not a marketing book, pricing and marketing are definitely interrelated issues. Therefore, I do offer many ideas concerning sales, marketing, diversifying, business ethics and artistic growth as they all relate to the subject of pricing.

Unintentionally defying stereotypes seems to be a pattern of mine. I am an artist, first and foremost. I think visually. My intelligence lies in perception. I always tested in the 99% percentile when it came to the math, logic and analytical-thinking portions of aptitude tests. Just thought you might like to know, considering that half the premise of this book is based on calculations; clear simple calculations designed to hopefully demystify the process of pricing artwork.

Because I am a painter, I refer to painting more often than not. I have tried to include as many other visual art mediums in the text of this book as possible. Please transliterate painter to weaver or sculptor or mixed-media artist whenever you need to. This way, any magnificent hybrid you create or tradition you follow will be included.

You will find that I use the term "your collectors" a lot. By collectors, I mean the people who buy your work. Anyone who owns two or more pieces of original artwork by one or more artists is a collector. The words buyer and customer are used on occasion as well. I don't like the term consumer, especially when it is used towards the general population. Consumer is like some kind of an anthro-zoomorphic vacuum cleaner. Look up the word consume as a verb. It's really interesting.

This book is geared towards the art market in North America, but only because this is my own experience. And I refer to US dollars since I have not had the good fortune to visit Mexico or Canada in recent years. I have traveled some in my life so far; Canada, England, Wales, Scotland, Mexico, Guatemala and Japan, and I look at art wherever I go. But the only place I know well is this place. I have been to 44 states as of this writing.

I have had the honor to know people from all over the world: friends, housemates, co-workers, classmates, fellow artists and now, family. I read voraciously, enjoy watching documentary films and I am generally aware of the world, as well as having a great respect for history. But I don't know enough about how it is for contemporary artists in other countries.

What I do know is that to some extent it is the same and different for artists the world over. It is the same for us because of the powerful creative urge, both spiritual and human, that we all have and share as visual artists. It is different due to the cultural, political and economic circumstances that vary throughout different times and places. And depending on the specifics of that time and place, artists might be highly exalted or severely oppressed, or anything in between. Those of us fortunate enough not to be suffering, to whatever degree, have an even greater responsibility to do our best as artists. We must do the best we can with our lives, and not waste our freedom of expression. It is way too valuable.

Meanwhile, basic math is true anywhere on the planet, even as perceptions towards artists and behavior of the markets vary and fluctuate. The mathematical portions of this book will be useful anywhere, as will many of the other ideas I have presented. They will just need to be adjusted to fit different circumstances.

And so I write from the point of view of an odd little imaginative girl who grew up with a dream, and who, over the years, has held onto that dream for dear life. I have arrived at this place in time with an intense case of keen reflection and observation. You see something wrong, something that needs changing, and so you fix it the best you know how, in your own context, using the very tools that you have on your shelf, as we continue to hunt and gather.

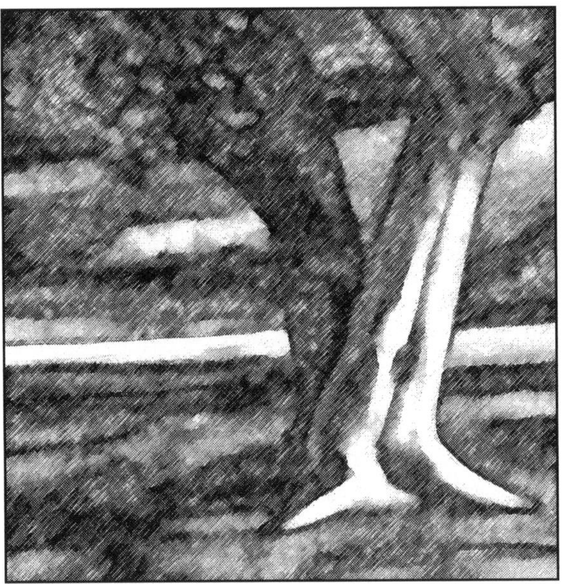

Pricing Rationale

Once upon a time, being the bohemian, struggling, punk-poor, young artist type, a little bit of money was a whole lot of money to me. I was a part of the "upper poor", as opposed to outright impoverished (in U.S. terms). Upper poor was fine; it was good enough, I didn't know any better and I was comfortable with it. It's not so awful if you're young and healthy, but it develops a bad romance to it in the long run.

For way too many years my pricing strategy had been; "just sell it", "at what price was I willing to part with it", "other poor artist pricing comparisons" and "whatever". I devalued myself quite frequently, because that is what I was taught to do. And yet I continued to give and give and give to the point where it was expected of me; real cash money, volunteer time, and free or really cheap artwork. I needed a serious pricing strategy, but I did not know that at the time.

Artists have all kinds of rationale for the way they price their artwork. Some of these are:

1. Ignorance. Many artists simply take a wild guess before pricing their work. They may go too high or too low, but either way, the only justification for their prices is sheer random guesswork. Prices for individual pieces of artwork change frequently in this category.

2. Pricing according to the buyer. The buyer decides how much they want to spend or can afford, and the artist accepts that price. Sometimes, the artist charges according to the financial status of the collector. Both are unethical. It is wrong to charge more to one person than to another for equal work. See the chapter on Consistency.

3. Desperation. This comes down to how much money an artist may need at the very moment, which makes selling a piece of art like going to the pawn shop to pay the bills. Financial desperation is no key to pricing. The value of your artwork will fluctuate, and this is no good for being thought of as a professional. See the chapter on Consistency for more on this subject. As broke as an artist may be at the moment (and I have known this all too well), do not become desperate. Desperation will drag you into poverty consciousness, which is difficult to leave behind.

4. The economy. Over the years I have often heard the argument that "now is a good time for artists to lower their prices", and this was well before the great recession. I do think it is always a good time to develop a separate body of work that costs less to create and therefore can be priced lower. However, it is never a good time to devalue your best art. Economies rise and fall, and then they rise again. I have been at this long enough to know firsthand that I have sold a consistent amount of paintings no matter what is going on in the economy. Stocks may fall, but unless someone actually drops that sculpture, it will not fall. Unless it becomes damaged, your work will not decrease in value. Therefore, do not devalue it. When times are good, put some money away into savings so that you may ride out the tough times. When times are tough, create good art that can sell at lower price points.

Keep consistant.

5. Clutter. This would be like selling your art cheap at a garage sale. Tempting sometimes, yes, I know. Do your prices go down when you are running out of space? Do they go up again when inventory goes down?

6. Sentimentality. Many artists will price work that they don't want to sell at an exorbitant price, thinking that no one will buy the piece. Doing this devalues any other work they may show, and if the price is way out of league with anything else, they will look foolish and/or arrogant. Plus, there are some collectors who will go straight for the most expensive piece. What happens if someone who can afford it decides to buy the work? What will you do then? Stating that a work is NFS (not for sale) is an option, as is not exhibiting a work of which you are very attached.

7. Arrogance. This results in pricing way above the value of your work, especially when it comes to quality, and especially in the earlier stages of your career. You may get lucky and actually sell some work for an unusually high amount. More likely, you will have to drop your prices significantly the next time around, which will not bode so well for your reputation. See the chapters called, "Consistency" and "The Variable Factors".

8. Insecurity. This is simply devaluing your hard work and creative vision. Again, see the chapter on variables. If you do not compare with others in terms of the quality and originality of your work, then now is as good a time as any to get better. True artists are constantly working to improve their skills. Do not feel bad about where you are at the moment. Just start from here, go forward and keep at it.

None of the above reasons are solid criteria for pricing your artwork. Each one is a reflection of amateur behavior. Serious artists would do best to leave all this behind.

The Calculations

There was this one nagging moment after this one particular exhibition when I began to sense that something was not quite. I wasn't all that sure I had actually made any money from the two sales I had at the reception.

So, a few days later I made a few lists and did a little math, and I soon realized that with most of my painting sales I was earning less than the federal minimum wage for my time. My share of the sale price after commission barely covered the cost and expense of creating the work, and sometimes not even that. There were times when not only did I not earn anything, but I was actually paying money out of my own pocket to sell my art. This was when I began to make extensive and accurate lists for myself as a painter.

Knowledge is Power

I already had complete records for material costs and business expenses directly related to being an artist. I had been keeping track of this information for tax purposes. I knew what money was going where and why. In early 1999 I began to keep track of time, the other part of the equation, which could then be divided into two components; time spent on the creation of each individual piece of artwork and time spent doing general support work. I knew that I spent a significant amount of time doing essential things besides painting at the easel. I just didn't know how much that was until I started recording the exact hours.

Knowledge is power. By keeping these records you will know how much work you actually do, and how much money you really spend on creating and sustaining your artwork. These numbers will help form and then legitimize your pricing structure.

About Overhead Expenses

Every pricing article and post that I have ever read excludes overhead when discussing both time and expense. Overhead means all the costs and expenses that go into the business of being an artist and creating your work, beyond the cost of the materials that go into individual pieces of art. Every article, it seems, has quoted "if a painting takes ten hours to complete and your materials cost $50..." or some variation on that theme. This is so incomplete! You spend more time and money than that, not just on the actual piece of artwork, but also on overhead and other support work involved with creating your work.

Compare this situation to other products and professions and businesses. Imagine if they didn't figure all their expenses and labor. What if restaurants only charged for the cost of the food and the chef's pay for cooking the meals? What about the time spent preparing the food? What about the costs of cookware, tables, chairs and kitchen equipment? What about heat, air conditioning, electricity, light bulbs, napkins, plates, menus, the wait staff, insurance, advertising and so on?

Imagine if your dentist, for example, only billed for x-rays, porcelain and the time he spent telling you it's okay to spit. What about the other people in the dental office doing essential support work? If you look around you will see a variety of medical supplies and tools, as well as an office full of things that have to be paid for in advance.

As an artist, you are a person in business and you have your share of overhead expenses. Once you start thinking about this and writing your own lists (see the next two chapters for details), you will see how much goes into your artwork that is not always apparent at first.

Calculating Costs for Figuring Overhead

The calculations that you do will let you know your exact material costs and business expenses. These two amounts equal the overhead that goes into each piece of art that you create.

If you have not already kept records and receipts of your material costs and business expenses, then begin now. Go through your studio space, darkroom, or wherever you create work and look around and list everything you have spent money on. Do this item by item. Go through your checkbook ledger and credit card statements. List all supplies, tools, equipment, insurance, books, workshops, etc. directly related to the business of being an artist.

If there are four rooms in your apartment and one is used exclusively as your art studio, then 25% of your rent, utilities and renter's insurance are considered a legitimate business expense. The same goes for a percentage of your car expenses. You will have to keep mileage records to calculate this amount.

The list you make will show you what goes into creating your art in terms of finances. Compare your list to mine in the next chapter, "What Goes Into a Painting". Going over my list will help you fill in some of the blanks on your list, although of course, your list will ultimately be your own.

Once you have your complete list, break up your materials and expenses into categories and make your own chart for Costs and Expenses. The one included below is only an example. You may need more columns. The one I actually use has 15 columns.

Work with only one year at a time; January 1st through December 31st. Add up the columns on each page, and then add up the sums from all the pages to get your annual totals. It's a lot of addition, but it's simple, especially with a calculator. Double-check each column to make sure your numbers are accurate.

There are other reasons to keep records of this information and to have these lists. Keeping accurate records of your costs and expenses makes it so much easier at tax time. All you have to do at the end of the year is add up your columns. Easy! These lists are also useful for keeping track of supply inventory for catalog shopping or if you need to put together a budget for a grant.

Costs and Expenses

I use a table, similar to this one, to record my costs and expenses related to being in business. You can create one of your own, print blank copies, punch holes, and place the pages in a binder. You can also buy one of those pale green ledger pads at the office supply store, if you don't want to create your own charts.

The amounts are recorded from receipts, checks, invoices, anything paid out as a business expense. I have included only four categories here as an example, and also as space permits.

Date	Item Detail	Supplies	Promo	Research	Rent
May 1	studio rent				300.00
May 4	museum admission			15.00	
May 4	postcards from museum			5.45	
May 7	oil paint	36.75			
May 8	gesso, varnish	19.60			
May 11	art photography		150.00		
May 12	promo postcards		39.20		
May 12	still-life props			8.50	
May 18	frames	62.00			
May 19	hardware and wire	17.85			

As a further example, my own cost and expense categories are; art supplies, tools and furniture, office supplies, postage and shipping, advertising and promotion, fees, dues, publications, research, workshops and classes, rent, phone (mobile account used for business travel only), travel and transportation, legal and professional services, and miscellaneous. I may not have expenses in every category in any given year, but over time, everything has been covered.

About Running Averages for Finding Overhead Expenses

From my records, I made lists of the previous five years' expenses. I then averaged my annual totals to get a better picture of what my general annual costs were. This is called a running average and is a more accurate way of calculating certain finances. In any one given year you may buy a lot of supplies and the following year you may buy fewer supplies, but you do not use everything the exact same year that you bought it. For example, over a period of five years you may spend $250, $375, $180, $220 and $315 on paint. Your running average for paint will be $268 per year.

You also need to consider your average creative output per year. Let's say that in most years you are able to complete 20 medium-sized paintings. However, last year you were only able to complete five paintings due to circumstances beyond your control. If your annual business expenses were around normal anyway, then do not average the five paintings as though you had done 20. Use the average overhead per painting cost from the previous year and apply that to those five paintings. This also why long-term cumulative averages work best. After a few years of record keeping you will get a feel for the general overhead expenses per piece of artwork you create.

When figuring running averages you do not have to do each item individually. Use your total business expenses; all material and studio costs, all your overhead expense for each year and do it that way. For example:

Year	Amount
Year One	$6,400.
Year Two	8,500.
Year Three	9,100.
Year Four	7,800.
Year Five	8,200.
TOTAL	$40,000.
5-Year Running Average	$8,000. per year

Maybe start monthly

The total for five years of expenses equals $40,000. Divide that total by the five years to get an average of $8,000 per year. The running part of the average comes in when you get to year number six. Let go of year number one and average in year number six, so that you will be working with the five most recently completed years.

If you do not have an accurate running average of costs and expenses for previous years, then use the total you have spent in the last year, and adjust the amount until it stabilizes in a few years. If you do not have running averages for general time spent doing support work, begin with one year's total amount. You may need to make a few estimations for future years based on what you remember of years past.

Two Other Issues in Considering Overhead

You may ask how does averaging in the costs of creating and exhibiting paintings A, B, and C affect the value of painting D, which has not been exhibited, but is still sitting in your studio? By exhibiting your work, even one piece at a time, you grow your career. This demonstrates that your art has enough value to be shown in a professional setting. Even if a certain painting isn't in a particular show, it could still sell. By putting effort into showing your artwork, the work on display could sell a piece in the studio. A good exhibit can bring people into your studio who may buy work not being exhibited at that time. This has happened to me on many occasions, and is an example of how everything you do goes into the averages.

Another thing to consider would be how to figure the overhead expenses for ten large time-consuming paintings, versus maybe 30 small studies, with both sets completed in the same year. They would not have the exact same overhead. With an $8,000 annual overhead one possibility would be to assign $500 per large finished painting and $100 per small study. Divide the overhead total amount equally if all the work you do is similar in size, materials and labor. Otherwise, apportion the amount in a way that makes sense to you, like the example just mentioned.

Time Sheets

There are two sets of time records that you will need to keep. They will let you know how much time you spend working. The Individual Artwork Time Sheets will tell you the exact time it takes to create each particular piece of art. The General Art-Related Work Time Sheets will help you calculate the average support time for each piece of art; whether those hours goes into the actual artwork such as bulk framing, or into increasing the value of your art such as the work that goes into exhibiting.

I keep both my blank and filled pages in a folder labeled PAINTING TIME SHEETS in my file cabinet. It's nothing fancy, but it works.

The Individual Artwork Time Sheet is for keeping track of the time you spend creating each individual piece of art. This is your time spent at the easel, the sculptor's pedestal, the potter's wheel, etc.

Think about your art-making process. Be very detailed. Write it out. Read what I wrote for my processes in the next chapter and translate that into your medium. Break it all down step by step. Everything you do on this list equals time you spend creating your artwork, whether it is working on an individual piece or general work done for a number of pieces at a time.

I used to set up two columns on my painting time sheets when I had two paintings going at once. Now I work on an average of four at a time. If you work on a number of individual pieces that overlap in time, you can set up multiple pages, and keep them in a binder. You can place older pages in the back of the binder and in a different section if you need to. Flip to the correct page when working on a particular piece. And yes, you can set this up on the computer in any format you are comfortable with. No special software needed.

If you work on multiples of artwork in one day; such as pottery, photography or print work, keep track of the total time. Then divide how many hours you spent all together by how many pieces you worked on that day. This way you will have an average of how much time it took to create that individual bowl, photograph or etching.

The General Art-Related Work Time Sheet is for keeping track of all the support work that you do. See my time/work/labor lists in the chapter called What Goes Into a Painting as an example. On this time sheet, you will keep track of the time you spend doing things such as buying supplies, varnishing, cutting mats, sending out invitations, and so on. This covers anything that goes into promoting your work as well as what you do to become a better artist, therefore increasing the value of your work. This also includes bulk work such as framing a dozen monotypes at once.

Go outside the time you spend in the studio and think about everything else you do that is a part of being an artist. Use my lists as an example. This would be everything you do from cleaning your tools to buying supplies to visiting museums to attending workshops to gathering information for these lists.

Following are examples of both time sheets; the Individual Artwork Time Sheet and the General Art-Related Work Time Sheet.

Individual Artwork Time Sheet

Date	Artwork	Hours
June 6	The Frozen Field	4.50
June 12	The Frozen Field	5.00
June 27	The Frozen Field	4.25
June 28	The Frozen Field	3.25
	TOTAL PAINTING TIME – The Frozen Field	**17.00 hrs**
July 3	The Steaming City	2.75
July 7	The Steaming City	4.00
July 12	The Steaming City	5.50
July 17	The Steaming City	6.00
August 2	The Steaming City	3.50
	TOTAL PAINTING TIME – The Steaming City	**21.75 hrs**

General Art-Related Work Time Sheet

Date	Activity	Hours
Sept. 4	Ordered supplies from online catalog	.75
Sept. 5	Cleaned studio, organized box of old slides	2.50
Sept. 12	Attend plein air workshop (including travel time)	7.00
Sept. 16	Scanned old slides, clean up images, organize jpegs	5.25
Sept. 19	Online research of galleries in neighboring state	1.75
Sept. 24	Built, stretched and gessoed eight canvases	4.00
Sept. 25	Second and third coat gesso, same canvases	1.50
Oct. 6	First Friday gallery hop	3.00
Oct. 11	Website updates	2.25
Oct. 14	Meeting with new curator at Art Center	1.00

A Living Wage

Another thing you need to do is calculate what a living wage is for you. A living wage is not the federal minimum wage, which decreases appallingly each year relative to the cost of living. A true living wage allows you to make a living. It will cover, in the equivalent of working 40 hours a week, all your basic living expenses. With a living wage you will neither starve nor luxuriate.

Make another list, this one for personal, non-business, expenses only. Use the sample Living Wage Checklist below if you like. You will only need to add or make changes to this as your own life circumstances change. This is just for your own information at the moment. Use a spreadsheet to create your own if you prefer.

List all your monthly personal, non-business, non-art-related expenses. If you are renting a four-room apartment and one room is your watercolor studio and you deduct 25% of your rent as a business expense, then 75% of your rent is a personal expense. The same goes for a percentage of your utilities, insurance and transportation expenses. Separate the two expenses;

business and personal. Your business-related expenses have already been covered in your overhead list/chart.

List all your necessary monthly personal expenses such as rent, mortgage, gas, electricity, water, other utilities, heating oil, phone, ISP, groceries, transit pass, car payment, car repair and maintenance, retirement fund payment, dental and medical co-payments, medicine, vitamins and all your insurance payments such as health, renter's or homeowner's, car and life insurance. Look at a few months of your checkbook and credit card statements to see what all your expenses are. If you have an annual payment on something, then figure your monthly average by dividing your annual payment by twelve months, or place it in the miscellaneous column.

Add a simple clothing and toiletry allowance, with a little weekly spending cash for incidentals. Keep it budget-minded and stick to the basics. Multiply any weekly expenses by 52 weeks per year to get an annual total, then divide that by twelve for a monthly average.

Do not add credit card payments to this list because those items that you charged are already either calculated into business expenses or into the above listed non-business expenses.

Do add expenses for raising a child and/or regular savings for that proverbial rainy day.

Don't add anything extravagant. That is what is meant by a living wage. If you want to dine at fancy restaurants, buy a brand new car every three years, or the latest electronic gadgets as soon as they come out, then you need to remember that these things are above the basics.

This may seem a bit harsh, or maybe not, but at the moment we are discussing your bottom line. You have the right to earn what you need to keep yourself alive, fed, clothed, housed, warm in winter and healthy enough to continue creating artwork. Nobody will have the right to argue with you concerning your bottom line. Everything else can be negotiated, considered profit, and/or discussed as a variable.

Calculating Your Living Wage

This chart is presented as an example only. These are not my expenses, and they may not be your expenses, but they are here as a template for you to use to make your own chart.

Personal Expenses	Weekly	Monthly	Annual	Misc.
Rent or mortgage, plus home insurance		800.		
Electricity, gas, water		125.		
Phone, internet		100.		
Car payment, auto insurance		205.		
Gas, repair, maintenance (estimated)		100.		
Automobile club membership			75.	
Health insurance premium		320.		
Co-pays and prescriptions (estimated)			250.	
Dental plan			130.	
Dental appointments (estimated)			400.	
Weekly groceries and household needs	50.			
Cash allowance (pocket money, clothing, etc.)	50.			
Retirement fund			500.	
Savings, emergencies, etc.			2,000.	
Estimated taxes (federal, state, local)				7,645.
TOTALS	100.	1,650.	3,355.	7,645.
Weekly expenses x 52 weeks	5200.			
Monthly expenses x 12 months		19,800.		
Total weekly, monthly, annual & misc expenses			36,000.	
Average monthly expense (annual ÷ 12)		3,000.		

The miscellaneous column is for bills that are paid on a quarterly, twice annually, or an every other month basis. Multiply by how many payments a year you need to make to get an annual figure. For example, a quarterly insurance bill of $200, would equal $800 a year if multiplied by four payments.

If you continue with the math, you will find that the annual $36,000 divided by 50 weeks (don't forget to omit your two weeks unpaid vacation) equals $720 a week before taxes. From there I divided by 40 hours to get an hourly figure, which is $18.00 per hour. Therefore $18 an hour is the living wage according to this example.

Math is Your Friend

Math is your good friend. This is really, truly, honestly basic and easy. It's not scary at all. Just list, add, multiply and divide. Take it one step at a time. All you need is a pad or some scrap paper, a working pen and a calculator. Set up your own charts or buy one of those pale green ledger pads and a cheap binder and you're all set.

Forget the rumors that real artists cannot do math. That's another stereotype meant to keep us from cluttering up our colorful little minds with supposedly mundane, yet complicated things. It's a lie. Artists use math all the time, just like we use carpentry and chemistry. Think of all the measuring you do. You will find that keeping track of your costs, expenses and hours is not so hard. Master this and you will have a wonderful sense of control. Math is your friend. Knowledge is power!

Don't forget to double-check all your figures. Go down one column and immediately go down that same column again. It will take a few minutes more, but you will then know that your figures are accurate.

If you truly are numbers-challenged, and some people are, then barter one of your other skills with a friend who can help you. Don't feel bad. Some of us who can do math easily leave prepositions lying all over the place, or whatever else we use to write with.

Putting it All Together

When you have completed your lists and tabulations and charts, and have made honest estimations for your time and expenses (if you don't have complete records already), you can then begin with the final calculations.

You should now have the following FOUR figures:

1. Your hourly living wage, based on your checklist and calculations
2. All your annual business costs and expenses, preferably as a five-year running average
3. The exact time spent on each individual piece of artwork (or average time spent on each piece in a batch)
4. Total annual time spent doing the necessary support work for your artwork and art career

Creating averages to refine the figures

Average your annual business costs and expenses. We will use the example of $8,000. Divide this amount by the 20 paintings that you complete in a year (also as an example), and this will come to $400 per painting. Therefore, the average overhead cost for each painting is $400.

See the previous sections concerning calculating overhead expenses in this chapter, for further details.

Support work is measured from the hours you record on your General Art-Related Work Time Sheets. Divide this amount by how many pieces you create in an average year. We will use the example of creating 20 paintings a year with 500 hours a year for support work. Divide 500 hours by 20 paintings and you get an average of 25 hours for each of those paintings spent preparing canvases, buying supplies, documenting the work, framing, going to the post office, and doing everything else on your support work list. This is your average support time per piece of artwork.

Now you should have the following four refined figures:

1. Your hourly living wage
2. Your overhead cost and expense per each piece of artwork
3. The exact time spent on each individual piece of artwork (or average time spent on each piece in a batch)
4. Your average time spent doing necessary support work for each piece of artwork

If you work on your art less than 40 hours a week, the above figures will still work for you. The 40 hours a week figure, which is basic full-time, is only for calculating your hourly living wage. If you spend 25 hours a week on your art, then you will need to spend another 15 hours a week doing something else on a part-time basis. If your totals are based on working as an artist 25 hours a week, versus 40 hours a week, your total costs and expenses would be proportionately lower as well, than they would for a full-time artist. You would spend more money and time to create more artwork at 40 hours, than for 25 hours, and it will average out more or less the same.

Chances are, you will probably not immediately sell all the work you create in any given year, but that is your issue, not your customers. There are ways to make up the difference, if not now, then later on. You will probably continue to sell work in any given year that was created in previous years as well. The time will come that you will earn a profit (more on that in a bit) on the work that you do sell. Meanwhile, outside work with a higher hourly wage, teaching a night class, or working on your art more than 40 hours a week total; all these things can make up for artwork not sold, yet budgeted. See the chapter on Growth for more ideas and options.

Continuing with the following four refined figures:

1. Your hourly living wage

   Example: $18. per hour

2. Your overhead cost and expense per each piece of artwork

   Example: $400. per painting

3. The exact time spent on each individual piece of artwork (or average time spent on each piece in a batch).

   Example: The painting titled; "The Frozen Field" took 17 hours to complete in actual painting time

4. Your average time spent doing necessary support work for each piece of artwork.

   Example: 25 hours per painting

Calculating the actual cost in five easy steps

1. The painting titled "The Frozen Field" took 17 hours at the easel to complete.
2. Add 25 hours of support work for a total of 42 hours to create the painting; from the initial creative thought to a varnished, framed and documented painting ready for exhibition and sale.
3. These 42 hours of labor paid at $18 per hour equals $756. This amount covers the total labor (the time spent) for creating this particular painting.
4. Add to this amount the overhead cost per painting, the money that was spent to create it, which is $400.
5. Therefore, $400 in overhead expenses plus $756 in labor equals $1,156. This is the actual cost to the artist to create the painting titled "The Frozen Field".

No Time Like the Present

There is no time like the present. Begin now, even if it is the middle of the year. Three years from now it will still be three years from now no matter what you have or haven't done between now and then. You may as well start now and be prepared. Estimate as best you can with the time averages based on the work you do now and continue with the next month and the month after that and so on. It is better to make an educated guess that is a little on the low side. It will be better to raise your prices later on, than to have to lower them.

By going through this process you will know the actual cost for each piece of artwork you that create. By doing these calculations and keeping these records you will know all the material costs, other expenses, overhead, time and labor; in other words, everything that goes into each piece of artwork. You will then know the REAL cost for each piece to come into existence. Cost is your bottom line to break even. Any price that falls short of this and you will lose money. How much loss can you afford to take?

In my opinion, some loss is okay on rare occasion in exchange for an opportunity that offers you guaranteed serious career advancement. However, losing money is not okay on a regular basis, unless you have the economic support and freedom to not need to get paid.

Beyond the Bottom Line

Beyond your material costs and overhead expenses and labor, there are a few other issues to consider. These are:

1. Any commissions you pay to an agent, a dealer, a gallery or other exhibition space to sell your work, which could fluctuate. In one year I have paid commissions ranging from 50% to 33% to none. If you are able to price your work at a certain percentage above your cost, then commissions can be covered. The 20% profit (as an example) made from not paying a commission on one sale, can help cover paying a 50% commission during the next sale. The ideal situation is to be able to price your work so that retail is double your cost. In this case you will not lose money paying a 50% commission, and make an actual profit when you pay less commission. See the chapter on Raising Prices for more.

2. Profits. This is the money any regular business earns above the cost of doing business. This money is often used for business growth; acquiring a new piece of equipment, moving to a larger studio, or buying the perfect solid oak easel to replace ol' rickety. Profits can also be saved as a cushion for low-income years, which is never a bad idea.

3. You will need to factor in issues such as your career history, the quality of your work, originality and so on. This will be discussed in the chapter on Variables. These issues will affect the price of your work.

4. The reality of the art market, not the current economy, which fluctuates from year to year, but the more consistent ongoing market. This will also be discussed in the chapter on Variables.

A Few More Notes (in three paragraphs starting with 'This')

This cannot be said enough. You will not compromise or interfere with your creativity or your artistic spirit by paying attention to the business side of things. This is all about finding a way to support your creativity and artistic spirit. On the other hand, if you keep losing money with each sale, then you will eventually have a lot less of yourself to give for creating your art.

This may seem like a lot of math, list-making and record-keeping, and it is, but only in the very beginning. Once you do your living wage calculations, there will only be minor adjustments in the future as your own personal situation changes. All the other lists and charts need to be set up just once, and then it is simply a matter of keeping up with them. It really only takes a few minutes a day to record studio and office times, and no more than 15 to 20 minutes a week to record and file receipts. Once the initial work is done, the rest is simple. Decide that it is in your best interest to do this work. Decide that it will be easy, and it will be. Besides, it's always fun to smash stereotypes.

This is not a book about taxes and other legal issues. However, all these lists will come in very handy when you file your taxes. Consult the IRS or a good accountant concerning your taxes. Besides any potential tax issues, do not falsify your costs, expenses and times when you are doing your calculations. Truthfully, you want your costs, expenses and times to be as low as possible, without compromising the quality of your work or your career. The lower these things are, then the sooner you will reach a point where you will break even. And the sooner you break even, then the sooner you will be able to make a profit on the sale of your work. Be honest with yourself.

What Goes Into a Painting

There came a sharp moment, soon after I had sold two small paintings at a gallery exhibition in 1998, that I knew something was not quite right. It was one of those squirmy little inklings that find their way deep into your brain. I suspected that maybe, just maybe, I was not so much selling my artwork as I was giving it away.

I then decided to quantify exactly what went into my paintings in terms of money, time, labor, skill and experience. After creating my lists and doing some basic calculations, I discovered that, yes indeed, I was giving much of my work away. I knew right away that I needed to change both my thinking and my pricing structure. The cold, hard math let me know I was losing money with each sale I made. The creation of these lists let me know how hard-working and experienced I really was. Putting all of this together was an extraordinarily revealing process.

In this chapter are modified versions of the lists that I made for myself. They are geared towards my own processes, circumstances and particular oil painting methods of that time. I have included them for you to use as a template for your own lists. In the following chapter, I have written material lists for various art mediums to use as a starting point, as well as instructions for creating the other lists for yourself. Besides self-knowledge, these lists are very beneficial for any artist to have, in case anyone argues with you about your prices, or your discount and donation policies.

Because I am primarily an oil painter my lists for this medium are extensive, although other oil painters will probably have somewhat different material and process lists from mine. Please note that any these lists may not be complete, but are there to start you on your way. As an artist who knows your own processes well, you can complete them yourself and adjust them to fit your own needs.

Note: I have recently begun a whole new body of abstract work, which is a somewhat different process than my previous body of representational work. These particular lists are based on that previous body of work, examples of which can still be seen on my website (www.alexalev.com) under the categories of stuffed critters and still-lifes. Also, replace any mention of slides and/or film with digital images.

Monetary Expenses

Art supplies

Oil paints
Gesso
Varnishes
Mineral spirits
Stand oil
PVA size
Masonite panels
Unfinished solid wood frames
Acrylic paint for frames
Wax medium for frames
Gold, silver leaf for frames
Canvas and stretcher bars

Tools and studio supplies

Painting brushes
Gesso and varnish brushes
Hardware
Hand tools; all basic tools
Power tools; sander, drill, saw
Staple gun and staples
Framing gun and points
Rubber gloves
Paper towels
Palettes

Mahl stick
Sandpaper, emery boards
Packing and crating materials

Studio

Furniture: tables, stools, bookcases, storage units
Easel
Color-corrected floodlights, fixtures, extension cords
Air purifier, replacement filters
Coverings to protect floor
Window coverings
Studio rent and utilities

Research materials

Props for still-lifes
Books, magazines, other pictorial materials
Film and development of photos for visual reference
Museum and other exhibition admissions

Career expenses

Slide and print photography
Slide duplicates, slide sleeves
Postcards, business cards, brochures
Invitations for independent exhibits and receptions
Any other advertising and promotional expenses
Monthly fees for ISP and web hosting
Jury and exhibition hanging fees
Organization dues and membership fees
Career-related books, magazines and publications
Related computer expenses
Office rent and utilities
Related office supplies and expenses
Desk, chair, lamp, bookcase, file cabinet, file folders
Postage, shipping and insurance
Photocopies of all paperwork

Travel

Transportation; local and long-distance
Hotels
Meals
Car rental

Miscellaneous

Related car expenses and/or public transportation
Art insurance
Disability insurance
Storage rent
Business-related phone calls
Business credit card interest
Workshops and classes

Note: Figurative painters will have model fees. Plein air painters have another list of expenses for painting in the outdoors.

Time/Work/Labor Issues Related to Art-making

Support work for creating art

1. Setting up, organizing and cleaning the studio space
2. Shopping for tools and other studio needs
3. Shopping for art supplies in stores, catalogs and online
4. Shopping for hardware, lumber, other painting support and framing supplies
5. Shopping for still-life props at antique, thrift, hobby and fabric stores, and produce, flower and flea markets
6. Shopping for books, magazines, and other visual art resources and references
7. Reading books, magazines, and other art publications
8. Shooting, printing and organizing reference photographs
9. Sketching as a resource for paintings

10. Visiting museums, galleries and other exhibitions to look at art, study various techniques and gather inspiration
11. Travel to out-of-state museums; making reservations, planning the trip, packing and actually traveling
12. Socializing and networking with other artists at receptions, other art events and independently
13. Attending classes and workshops for upgrading technical skills and exploring new methods and mediums

Actual process for creating oil paintings on hardboard panels:

1. Sand and prime a small group of panels at once
2. Set up still-lifes
3. Set up and mark lighting
4. Preliminary drawing
5. Actually paint. Wow*
6. Daily cleanup of brushes and workspace
7. When paintings are completely done, put away still life props
8. Safely store and catalogue paintings
9. Order wood frames
10. Prepare frames; patch, sand, paint, gild, varnish, and/or wax and buff
11. Varnish the painting when it is six months old. If the painting needs to go on exhibition before that, then apply retouching varnish (after one month)
12. Frame (drill, wire, etc.) the painting for exhibiting, or safely store for future sale and/or exhibition

* In all of these lists and sub-lists, see how little time is spent on "actually paint". During my good years I have found that I spend about 2/5ths of my time sitting at the easel and about 3/5ths of my time doing everything else. On the expense list, see how few items are actually art supplies.

Time/Work/Labor Related to Business Issues

Examples of business-related things professional artists must do

1. Promotional work for adding value to the artwork and to the artist's name
2. Promotional work for gaining sales opportunities
3. Paperwork involved with exhibition, sales, grants, etc.
4. Research for gaining knowledge and information concerning various art career opportunities
5. Preparation and filing of copyrights annually for all new work

Career-related research

1. Shopping for books, magazines and other art-career resources
2. Reading books, magazines and other art-career publications
3. Researching exhibition, grant, residency, publication and other opportunities
4. Researching galleries via print resources and online
5. Researching photographers, framers and other suppliers
6. Networking with other artists and art-career people
7. Attending classes and workshops related to art-career issues
8. Travel to research galleries; reservations, planning, packing, actual travel time
9. Appointments and meetings with potential dealers, galleries and collectors

After a painting is finished in the studio (for promotional purposes, exhibition and sale)

1. Photographing paintings for slides and prints. This must be done before varnishing the work. Bring and retrieve paintings, pack and wrap them for safe transport, approve the slides
2. Ordering slide duplicates
3. Organizing slides in an archival storage system
4. Ordering prints and/or postcards

5. Wrapping, packing, moving, crating, storing, insuring paintings; depending on what happens next in the life of the painting

Note: I don't know about you, but I love the world of digital imagery. Slides be gone! Of course, digital images still need organizing and optimizing, and they still need to be photographed or scanned in the first place.

If there are sales

1. Bills of sale (with notification of copyright, etc.) need to be written, filled out and signed
2. Packing, moving, crating if the sale is not local
3. Dealing with a cancelled sale: legal, financial, whatever

The process involved with applying to exhibitions, galleries, grants, etc.

1. Call or send an SASE for the prospectus, application procedure, and/or application form
2. Wait for, and then fill out the application form
3. Make a copy to keep as a record
4. And/or all of the above in digital form with an online application, each of which is a different process from the next one
5. Decide on which images to submit
6. Check availability and condition of artwork for submission
7. Complete process of entry form, each one different from the next
8. Update resume
9. Write or update statement
10. Maybe write a cover letter, depending on the situation
11. Prepare an SASE for the return of materials, if necessary
12. Go to the post office, wait in line
13. Follow-up and/or wait for a response
14. If the jurying process is not from images, but from actual work, then the artwork must be driven to the exhibition site, and if the work is not accepted, it must be picked up again a few days later.

15. If all or any of the paintings are accepted, then some or all of the following work must be completed: paperwork, press-releases, interviews, preparing images for promo, sending invitations, mailing list, phone calls, delivering the work. If shipping paintings, then dealing with shippers, packing materials and more paperwork. Attending the reception, if possible, depending on distance and weather. Give an artist talk, slide lecture or PowerPoint presentation, community outreach, and so on.

Miscellaneous paperwork

1. Federal, state, local and sales (or gross receipts) tax paperwork
2. General record keeping; sales, expenses, inventory, all time sheets
3. Organizing files, and keeping them organized
4. Designing invitations and other promotional materials
5. Filing copyrights; organizing and labeling slides, typing and copying Form VA, preparing packet and mailing
6. Any other paperwork not listed here
7. Miscellaneous art-related mail, e-mail, phone and fax communications
8. Shopping for office and shipping supplies

Experience and Background as an Artist

In this section I will be using myself as an example. Do this for yourself, as well. All this background; the time, effort, energy, skill-building, exploration and creativity that you put into your work and art career over the years add value to what you do. These things count for much.

General experience and career history

1. Painting in watercolor and acrylic since 1975
2. Painting in oil since 1977
3. Exhibiting since 1981, both solo and group
4. Attended Massachusetts College of Art
5. Graduated with honors from the San Francisco Art Institute
6. Grants, awards, lectures, publications, reviews, sales, etc.

7. Teaching at various art centers, private creative advising, coordinating exhibitions for other artists
8. See five-page resume for details. Short-version resume is on my website.

None of this means anything if I don't have the goods

My work must be of high technical quality and have originality of vision to be worth it.

Level of Technical Skill, Creativity, Originality

How does one judge this?

1. Look at my work with an educated eye
2. Let me critique or discuss someone else's work

Number one – My background as a painter

Painting skill is a growth process. I have been at this for a very long time, developing my own unique and original vision. I have spent the same number of years developing my technical abilities. I am still continuing the growth process, not ever being completely satisfied. This is the thrill of the hunt.

Besides my earliest explorations in paint as a teenager, plus two sets of student work from two different art schools, I have created four solid bodies of strong, distinct work so far, all totaling over 500 finished paintings. Imagine all the unfinished ones, and there were plenty. I must have learned something along the way, especially considering that I am brave enough (as some folks say) to shift directions when one thing has played itself out after so many years. The four solid bodies of work lasted for seven years, then eight years, then fourteen years, and the current one is eight years and counting (there was some overlap with the previous set). Just so you know I am not a flake, drifting from one thing to the next with no rhyme or reason.

I have a decent range of professional accomplishments. See the above points in General Experience and Career History, and the length of my resume. This demonstrates that there are other people in the position of deciding these things who believe that my artwork has some value.

Number one, as well – Look at my work

That's right. Look at my work. Look at it with an educated eye and understanding of paint handling, color, composition, subject matter, allegory, etc. See, I have it covered. Look at my work with an open mind if you don't have a background in art. Does it move you, do you find it interesting to look at, intriguing to think about? Would you want to have it around? Compared to what is out there, there isn't much else quite like it, in any of the four bodies of work I have created so far.

Every painting I do now has 500 paintings of actual experience behind it, in at least 39 years. I have studied intensively, paid attention to art history, paid attention to the contemporary art world, and not just in colleges and workshops. My predominant mode of education is consistent self-study at museums and other exhibitions, books, observation of nature, experimentation in materials and ideas, not being lazy at the easel and most importantly, keeping at it over the years no matter what.

Number two - Intelligent critiquing

Over time I have developed the ability to honestly and clearly critique paintings. I can see composition, color, drawing, lighting, line and mass. I can see these things as separate elements, and I can see them as a whole. I can see content; emotional, sensual, verbal and non-verbal, intellectual, historical and that which is timeless. As most former art students, I have a basic grasp of at history. I also have an above-average understanding of science and general history. I can filter out my own artistic vision and be quite objective if need be. I can be very subjective as well.

My skills have been tested as a painting teacher in the classroom, as well as more informal settings. I am able to assist other painters when they are stuck or are having difficulties with a particular painting or with painting in general. My efforts almost always get straight to the point, and they are always greatly appreciated. This is a natural skill that I have had for years.

Now, a lot of people teach and critique and curate and judge, and some of them are not all that good at it (although of course, many others are quite excellent at what they do), so this is a flawed criteria. Observation by another objective person might be necessary to prove these abilities. But what is it that decides objectivity? This could go on and on. Or maybe someone who is willing to be an open subject for another, by doing so, then gives proof of objectivity. Maybe. It all depends... Chase that tail!

A Few More Words

Putting all this together was immensely revealing to me. Make comparable lists and statements for yourself. It's a very empowering process to go through. You will learn so much and have a greater sense of clarity concerning all the work that you do as an artist.

What Goes Into Other Mediums

On these pages I have compiled some of the materials, tools and other items that you might use in creating your art, depending on your medium. The following lists are given only as examples. Use them as a starting point for your own lists. I have filled them in as best as I could, and I apologize if I mention anything idiotic. I am familiar with many of these methods, having tried a few through classes or my own dabbling. I also have artist friends for whom any of these might be their medium of choice, so I have some idea as to what many of these material lists would include. There are probably some things that I have left out, although not intentionally. I know painting, and I know my own processes of painting intimately. I will assume that you know what you do quite well, too. See the chapter on Calculations for more information on how to fill out your own complete materials list.

I am aware there are also many other visual arts mediums, and variations on visual arts mediums, as well as unlimited hybrids of visual arts mediums combined. Use my thorough oil painting list, as well as the materials compilations from any other medium as a basis to create your own list. Again, I have included these as examples only.

How to Make Your Own Materials and Expenses Lists

Make a complete inventory list of all the materials that you use in making your art. Look at each piece and dissect it, examining each component that you put into your work. Then see what other materials you have in your studio, on your worktables, and behind cabinet doors. List all the materials that actually go into your artwork.

Make a complete list of the overhead costs of making your art. This would include some of the following items and expenses: All expenses for maintaining a studio, separate or in the home, such as rent, utilities, lighting, furniture, ventilation, tools and equipment. Add the costs of gathering ideas, inspiration, research, education, tuition, classes, workshops, residencies, museum admissions and art books. Include all finishing processes to prepare your work for sale and exhibition, plus documentation, framing and promotional expenses.

How to Create Your Own Time and Labor Lists

Make a complete list of your own art-making processes. Write down exactly what you do to create an individual piece of art, one step at a time. Begin with germinating an idea and end with preparing the piece for sale, exhibition or archival storage.

Make a complete list of the support work that you do. This would include things like the time spent buying supplies, getting your work photographed, researching exhibition possibilities and so on. See what I wrote on my oil painting lists under this category, and adjust it to your own needs. Add and subtract the things that you do in particular, or don't do, as a working artist in creating a larger, or new, body of work.

In summary, you want to make complete lists for the following four items:

1. Supplies

   The cost of the materials that go into your artwork

2. Expenses

   The overhead cost of being an artist and creating a body of work

3. Process

   The direct labor that goes into each individual piece of artwork

4. Support work

   The indirect labor that goes into being an artist, for the purposes of creating, exhibiting and selling your artwork

The Tools and Materials Lists

Acrylic paints

Paint from the tube and/or jar, gesso, gel mediums, texture gels, glazing liquids, acrylic varnishes, painting surfaces (canvas, panel, paper, etc.), framing materials, brushes, palette knives, hard palette or palette paper, rags and/or paper towels, easel

Watercolors

Paint from the tube and/or cake, watercolor paper and journals, brushes, palettes, painting trays or ceramic watercolor dishes, palette cups (for water), masking fluid, matting and framing materials, tissues and/or paper towels, accessories for keeping or cleaning brushes, paint boxes, watercolor carryalls (for painting out of studio), your easel and/or other work surfaces

Pastels and drawing

Pencils, charcoal, graphite sticks, pastels (hard, soft and/or oil pastels), drawing inks, markers, paper, journals, calligraphy tools, blending tools, knife, sharpener, blades, paper stumps, tortillions, pastel and charcoal extending tools, fixatives, erasers, mat board, framing materials, boxes for keeping materials, folders, portfolios and archival storage boxes for keeping finished drawings, drawing boards, accessories for painting outside the studio

Traditional photography

Film, paper for printing, chemicals for developing and printing, enlarger, darkroom tools, timer, red light and enlarger bulbs, cropping tools, filters, lenses, lupes, cotton gloves, gray card, matting and framing materials, sleeves for negatives, folders, portfolios and archival storage boxes, camera, camera bag, tripod

Digital arts

Computer and peripherals (monitor, scanner, printer, etc.), software, ink cartridges, things to scan, paper for printing, all framing and presentation materials, folders, portfolios, archival storage boxes

Mixed-media

Look at everything you have ever created, piece by piece, and list everything that has gone into your finished mixed-media artwork. The below is an example of such a list for mixed-media acrylic painting assemblage.

Wood panels, wood trim, sandpaper, gesso, modeling paste, acrylic paints, gel mediums, textured gels, beads, decorative nails, lengths of chain, buttons, ribbon, feathers, wire, screw eyes, wood glue, craft glue, paint brushes, palette knives, wire cutters, pliers, hammer, scissors

Printmaking – general

Inks, paper, all appropriate chemicals for the particular printmaking medium, all appropriate tools for the particular printmaking process, cleaning supplies, drying racks, all matting and framing materials, folders, portfolios, archival storage boxes

Etching

Etching inks, dry pigments, printing paper, zinc and copper plates, etching ground, etching solution, asphaltum, plate oil, plate cleaner, intaglio tools, gravers, burnishers, scrapers, brayer, tarlatan, blotting paper, etching press, wool blankets for the press

Linoleum and woodblock printing

Block printing inks, paper for printing, linoleum blocks (or wood blocks for woodcuts), linoleum cutting knives, knife handles, blades, brayer, baren, surface for rolling out inks

Silkscreen

Inks, squeegee, printing paper, resist, silkscreen (frames and screens)

Lithography

Lithography inks, paper, limestone and aluminum plates, lithography crayons, sponges, asphaltum, gum arabic, levigator, lithography press

Ceramics

Clay, stoneware, porcelain, glazes, brushes, sponges, wire cutter, slab rollers, wedging board, clay tools, palettes, scrapers, finishing tools, wheel, kiln, heat-resistant gloves, stilts, cones, ware racks.

Clay sculpture

Clay, armature wire, modeling tools, hardwood tools, palettes, calipers, scrapers, rasps, canvas, pedestal, turntable and stand

Stone sculpture

Stone, beeswax, marble wax, marble polish, carving chisels, hammers, calipers, all other tools, buffing wheels, sandbags, hydraulic table cart

Wood sculpture

Wood, tools, knives, mallets, sandpaper, sanding tools, saws, other equipment

Metal sculpture

Metal sheets, rods, wire, safety equipment, protective clothing, welder's goggles, arc welders, soldering equipment, chisels, pliers, all tools, gas, use of foundry for casting, use of any metal shop

Stained glass

Glass sheets, bevels, ornaments, medallions, metal foils, solder, copper wire, lead, glass cutters, saws, blades, safety glasses, solder iron, iron tips and cleaner, window frames, lamp bases, other lamp parts, including electrical parts

Lampwork (glass)

Glass rods, strips, color powders, torch, cutting tools, pliers, clamps, scoring knives, glass grabbers, grippers, tweezers, pressing tools, shaping tools, safety goggles

Weaving

Yarn, ribbons, cords, other materials used in weaving, dyes, spinning wheels, carders, spindles, clippers, shuttles, bobbins, winders, hook, reeds, loom benches, table and other looms

Quilting

Fabric, thread, buttons, trim, ribbon, bias tape, batting, marking tools, rotary cutters, rulers, grids, cutting mats, hoops, frames, hand and machine needles, sewing machine

Giving It Away

We give it away quite often: our time, our expertise, our creative output. Some of what we give away, we give sincerely from the heart, soul and mind – and this good. We help to make the world go round, especially when giving feels right to us. It is always a good thing to take the time and effort to inspire younger artists, do some community work, share information, contribute the occasional piece of work, help another artist, reach back and lend a hand – all of this at no cost sometimes, and other times by giving excellent value for what is paid for in full.

However...

Some time ago, I read an article in one of the west coast weekly papers about why art should be free. Not free as in uncensored or free of inhibitions, but free, 100% discount free, no price tag free. The premise was that art is something essential to culture and society, belongs to the whole of humanity, and therefore how could one put a price tag on it. Art belongs to everybody. The final production of objects and ideas by artists should be free. That's right. Free. Paintings, drawings, mixed-media sculpture, whatever it is that you create, just give it away, because everybody else has a right to own your art.

The author of that article didn't mention the production and service of any other profession or vocation... just that visual artists are responsible for supplying society for free with the fruits of their creation. We owe it because realized creativity is essential to the spiritual and intellectual well-being of everyone. We should just be thankful that we have the ability to create.

Argh! Exclamation point!

Well, until my housing, medical care, groceries and whatever else I need are given to me for free then I'm not giving my work away, unless I choose to completely of my own free will. No more guilt! Artists as a group are usually sensitive and generous, and we are often easily made to feel guilty by such arguments. We get hit on from all angles. I mean, should we starve, or continue to starve, because it fits someone else's stereotype of how artists should live?

Why should ownership be free, if the viewing of artwork is already free in most circumstances? Should ownership of anything be free? How much is too much ownership, as in how is equal ownership of free artwork going to be regulated? Or is some ownership more equal than others? What do the artists get for free in this situation, besides the feeling of being used?

Exhibiting for Free

The main thing that artists do for free is exhibiting their artwork. Free, meaning: free-to-the-public for viewing purposes. It is not free to the artists who exhibit, nor is it usually free to the exhibition space.

Galleries are usually free to wander into. There are multitudes of non-commercial and non-profit exhibition venues that are open to the public such as community art centers, libraries, college and university galleries, and so on. Outdoor crafts festivals often have free admission, or there might be an arts exhibition building that is part of a major fair where general admission is paid for other reasons. Most museums offer a regularly scheduled free day or evening where anyone may enter without paying. Plus, there are many other indoor and outdoor events and festivals, as well as spontaneous happenings, that are open to all without paid admission.

Yes, the artwork is often for sale, but there are no guarantees that anything will sell, or that enough pieces will sell to sufficiently cover all the costs involved with exhibiting. Plus, a person does not have to buy anything to enjoy looking at the artwork or to gather inspiration.

Public art is publicly owned, therefore of course, it is owned by everyone. Purchased with public funds, artists are usually paid for this work, sometimes well, sometimes not. Public art is always free for viewing. Plus, everyone owns it. Non-public art is almost always free at some point for viewing, as opposed to owning. If you personally own a piece, the main reason to do so is to be able to view it at anytime. Of course, there is a big difference between having a beloved painting hanging in your own home where it may inspire you and your family for generations, or seeing a painting once or twice at an exhibition surrounded by other people. But it is usually free to see that painting the first or second time around.

Non-Profit Exhibiting

Many exhibitions are presented for educational and cultural purposes only, often with a specific theme, and if any sales come as a result, it is purely accidental. I have participated in quite a few of these exhibitions. Sales are not the goal. Many artists lend their artwork, and give their time and effort to see that these shows are a success in reaching many people.

I participated for three years in a wonderful project in San Francisco involving room-sized installations for the Day of the Dead holiday. This was the educational and inspirational brainchild of a professional curator who was a joy to work with. I created a room myself for two years at the Mission Cultural Center, and one year as a two-person collaboration at the Yerba Buena Center for the Arts. I did painting-based installation projects. This meant that I brought in about four to six months' worth of paintings to start. Then, I built the installation around them, including painting the walls, constructing ceilings, collecting extensive installation materials and placing, gluing, hammering, and tying lots and lots of things together. Then I would create all kinds of signage, since I was big on text.

Only in my third installation were the artists given a $50 stipend per room, of which we were most grateful. (The previous venue did not have the funds.) I collaborated equally with another artist, a talented sculptor, on this particular room, and we decided to use the money on some of the shared materials. However, this stipend covered only a fraction of our costs.

Most of the artists I observed or spoke with during my three different years with this project gave between three and seven looooong days of their time, plus weeks or months in planning and up to a few hundred dollars in materials for each room, each year, out of their own pockets. Nothing was for sale, and except for that $50 stipend, nothing was paid to any artist. It was a ton of fun to create, two tons of hard work and a tremendous gift to the people of the Bay Area. Thousands of people visited the completed rooms each year and were touched deeply by many of the unique and powerful installations.

There are countless public community-based projects all over the country that pair local artists with neighborhood groups to create public artworks and/or events. Artists often go unpaid, or are severely underpaid, but do this as a gift and because it is often a fun and sociable thing to do, and maybe the cause is worthwhile to them as well. However, they are usually not financially compensated very well, if at all, and these sorts of endeavors usually result in free art for the public to enjoy.

The Costs of Exhibiting

It costs to exhibit. See the chapter called What Goes Into a Painting for details. Some of those costs may be recouped via sales, but there are no guarantees. All the money that it takes to exhibit, except for any sales commission, is paid up front. Temporary installation projects and other new-genre works, by their very physical nature, cannot usually be sold, and therefore those artists do not even have much of a chance of being compensated at all. Artists are rarely paid a stipend to exhibit. In fact, more and more artists are paying fees to display their work. This is not like a performance where you are paid for your services. We exhibit for free.

Consider shipping costs, as an example. I remember being part of an exhibition that included entries from all over the country. This particular gallery always had interesting group shows. The owner pointed out a painting by an out-of-state artist to me, since even she was perplexed concerning the situation. The painting was rather large and priced at only $400, which was the artist's chosen price (which is often done in juried group shows). Now, the gallery took a 40% commission on sales, and had a $15 jury fee. So, if the painting did sell, we are looking at a retail price of $400, less $160 (the 40% commission), less the $15 jury fee for an artist's commission of $225. Because of the size of the painting and the distance, the artist easily spent $100 on shipping, leaving a balance of $125 for the artist for the sale. With all the other costs and the labor involved with creating the painting, we are now looking at not very much of anything, if anything at all, for the artist and that is only if the piece actually sold.

Artists often create promotional giveaways, such as postcards, full-color show announcements and invitations, which in essence are free art reproductions. This giveaway is really okay. It's promo. I am truly honored when people tack, tape and sometimes frame my postcards and hang them up. I thoroughly understand when someone cannot afford an actual painting because of tight finances. It happens. I wish they could buy my paintings. I wish I could bring my prices down, but since I also desire to continue painting (and living indoors) we just have to wait until their financial situations get better. This happens too.

Concerning what it costs to exhibit, I am fine with presenting my work to an audience that predominantly will not be buying. It is my gift. I much prefer it when sales are made, but that is not my sole criteria for exhibiting. Artists need money, but we also need to show our work. It's part of what we do.

Open Studios

Open studios are a major gift that artists give to their local communities. These weekend events are usually free to the public, whether they are municipality-based or privately sponsored. They can be a lot of fun and can also be a good career opportunity for the artist. However, opening your studio to the public is also a significant amount of hard work. Generally speaking, less-expensive items and reproductions sell more easily at these events, if anything sells, but there are always exceptions.

Above and beyond the costs of creating the artwork and the usual overhead, there are extra expenses, time and labor involved with open studios. There are often hefty entry fees (at least participation is guaranteed), the production of special presentation materials such as framing, portfolio books, guest books, a special run of business cards, postcards and/or other promotional giveaways, the printing and mailing of invitations, and refreshments.

Time is spent creating these materials, cleaning and rearranging the studio for visitors, shopping for snacks and drinks, and afterwards more time is spent putting things back in working order after the event.

Then there is the time spent actually hosting the open studio. This can be anywhere from a solitary evening event to a three-day weekend with long hours. Open studios, in most cases, are both an enjoyable and exhausting gift that artists give to the public.

Loans and Rentals

Artists are sometimes called upon to offer loans of artwork, sometimes called exhibiting with the promise of exposure and potential sales. These situations are often in people's private homes, offices and corridors, and other businesses. Sometimes no sale label is posted, there is no publicity and no reception. In my experience, the people who have the loaned artwork on their walls forget that it is for sale and everyone else figures that it just belongs there. This is called a free loan. There is no benefit to the artist other than storage. It should be a paid rental.

There are a few enlightened museums and galleries around the country that do rent artwork. I was fortunate to be associated with one of the best when I lived in California; the San Francisco Museum of Modern Art Rental Gallery. Both the museum gallery and their clientele understood that art has real value. And if you chose not to buy, renting was an option. The artists were paid a small (but very reasonable) fee for having their work on loan, and the small checks certainly added up. Plus, the art patrons were able to have a changing display of art in their home or office.

Donations

As a percentage, and especially in relation to the ability of many of us to be able to afford to give something away, it seems that artists get asked to donate to auctions, benefits and fund-raisers an extraordinarily disproportionate amount of the time compared to other professions. Ask any artist. Of course, this may only be a matter of perception.

The people who attend these auctions and benefits often have disposable income, and they get something in return for participating in the fund-raiser. The artist, not so much (in most cases).

I sometimes suspect that artists are approached for donations because of the hobby attitude. If the art produced is simply extra stuff, made in one's spare time, a hobby instead of a vocation, it is something done just for the fun of it and this makes it okay to give away. They say to the artists "You have so much of it lying around. You can spare something, no problem".

Why is what we do so valued in one way and so devalued in another? Almost everyone wants original art in their homes, yet so many are not willing to pay for what it actually costs to create. There are people who will spend significant amounts of money on ephemeral things such as gourmet meals, designer-label clothing, or a shiny new car every few years, but squirm mightily about paying for something that will last for generations, will neither wear out nor go out of style, and will most likely increase in value over the years.

There will come a point where the artist cannot afford to continue being so nice.

If artists are continually giving away work, then how are their own basic needs going to be met? How will they purchase art supplies? If an artist is not able to pay the bills or buy groceries, that artist will go hungry, become homeless, and then have no place to create art or have the good health to continue to do so. There is no real glamour in artists living this way, despite the myth. Everybody loses.

Multiples such as photographs, prints, pieces from a pottery run are a little bit easier to give away, but still... Too many multiples of photos or prints can devalue a run. If too much of a multiple is given away then it is unfair to the collectors who paid full price for the same work and unfair to the artist who created it.

Donations – A Few of my Experiences

Between 1999 and 2005 I took part in an annual benefit exhibition and sale for the Albuquerque Museum in New Mexico called 'Miniatures', which was truly a pro-artist event. In fact, this fund-raiser was pro-everybody. The artwork was not given away by any means. It was fairly priced for both the artists and the collectors, with the prices being set by the artists. A reasonable commission of one-third of the sale price was slated for the museum foundation, which benefits both the arts and the larger community, and the artists received the balance of two-thirds. A sale of $1500 equaled $500 for the foundation and $1000 for the artist. This benefit exhibition was professional, well-organized and there was easy communication between the museum foundation and the artists. 'Miniatures' was a completely insured, prestigious, well-presented show in a lovely museum setting. They treated the artists like the professionals that we are, artists were paid within a few weeks of any sale and they expressed sincere gratitude for our participation. It should always be like this.

I've also had some very different experiences. I once took part in an auction at a downtown gallery. For a number of years they hosted an exhibition with a silent auction of the artwork. The artists would receive 50% of the sale price and the annual cause (which was different every year) would receive the other 50%.

The realities were a little different though, at least for me, since I create labor-intensive original work. When I first arrived with two small paintings, I was informed that the bidding would start at half of the comparable retail price. In other words, a painting of mine, which would normally sell for $1200, was set at a beginning bid of $600. I was not forewarned of this when I was invited and agreed to participate. The gallery assistant assured me that this was just to get the auction going, and that in nearly all cases the prices would go up, up, up, over and beyond the usual retail price.

I attended the reception and kept my eye on the bidding throughout the month of the exhibition. Very few of the bids went past a second bid. I ended up losing money on the two paintings (which sold), because I was receiving 25% of retail, when full retail barely equaled my cost for expenses and labor. In fact I paid about $500 out of my own pocket (just to cover my material costs and overhead) to have the two paintings sold, regardless of my labor.

A year or two earlier, I was approached by another organization to donate a large painting for a benefit auction. I told them that I could not afford to do so, but I would be happy to donate an earring and necklace set instead (I was doing a lot of beading at that time). This was for a cause that meant very little to me, and although I wasn't against it, I personally thought that there were much more important things out there to support. However, I was willing to give the one-of-a-kind jewelry set to help them out.

The person in charge acted very insulted by my counter-offer. She made a big thing about it only being just one painting when she spoke to me. Then she began to talk to other people about the uncooperative artists in the community. It seems I was not the only one giving her terrible trouble by not jumping at the chance to give some of my best work away for nothing. She wasn't even familiar with my art, let alone what it took to create it.

A more level-headed member of the organization then held a meeting with a few of the artists, and let us know that we could donate anything we wanted and it would be appreciated. We could even set a minimum bid for the purpose of receiving a small stipend. I asked for just enough to cover the costs of the beads, but not pay for my time. At the auction the jewelry set sold above the minimum bid, I received my few dollars and also a few more negative words concerning the situation from the original person. Instead of being pleased that someone wanted to wear one of my creations, I felt used by the experience.

Donations – Developing Your Own Policy

Remember that a percentage of the final selling price at an auction does not always equal getting paid for your time or even meeting material costs. Your work will probably be selling below retail, below wholesale, or even way below cost. In the long run, this is not fair to yourself or to your collectors who do pay full price. If you give away too much, and your artwork can often be purchased well below your regular prices, then why should anyone pay full price in your studio or through a gallery? You are not only protecting your immediate finances, but the long-term integrity of your career by limiting donations.

In my opinion, the best policy, especially for an artist who does only original one-of-a-kind, labor-intensive artwork would be to participate in one or two benefit/auction/donation situations a year. Period. Just say that this is your policy and that's that. Hold firm. Maybe you'll donate to a new cause next year, maybe not.

Always make sure that you donate to a cause that you truly want to support. Is the sponsoring organization respectful of the arts and the individual artists? Will you receive a small percentage? Is the cause reflective of your belief system? Is there fun involved? Is there any other benefit to you? Even if you lose money on the deal, and most likely you will, you need to somehow feel good about the donation.

If they tell you that you can take a tax deduction for your donation, remember that as of this writing, you can only take a charitable deduction if you file Schedule A with your taxes, which many of us don't qualify for. And then, as an artist, you can only deduct the actual cost of the exact materials used in that particular piece of artwork, and nothing else. Any other owner of a piece of artwork may deduct the full market value, but not the creator.

As this book edition goes into its final edit, we are still waiting for the law to change in favor of artists deducting the full value of their donated work. This is the Artist Fair Market Value legislation or act. You will need to check into this yourself to see if the law passed, if and when you donate any artwork now or in the future.

Beginning bids should reflect the general market value of the artists' work. If you donate a watercolor that would normally retail for $800 at that approximate size, then make sure that the beginning bid is at least three quarters of that price for a minimum of $600. You are choosing to give your artwork to them. Therefore, you are in control. If they disagree, they don't get your work. Get it in writing. People will understand that a beginning bid may be low, but you do not want it to be too low, giving the perception that your work is losing its value. Seventy-five percent is a good compromise between 50% and 100%.

If in the end, any stipend you receive is less than the cost to create the work; all overhead expenses, materials and all labor involved, then you are giving them the difference to auction your work. Remember that cost is your break-even point. Anything below that is money and/or labor you are giving away. If you receive a stipend, then it is probably just to help with expenses. Otherwise, you are paying them good cash money along with donating your work.

Do not ever give your work away only for the publicity. The exposure may do you some good, but don't count on it. Publicity may be a side benefit, but there is no guarantee that it will become of any use to you. If they promise you future rewards, such as exhibiting opportunities, sales or publicity, get the details in writing and have the papers signed by at least two officials of the sponsoring organization, in case one quits soon afterwards (this happens).

Giving It Away with the Help of Galleries

Some years ago, an artist I once knew congratulated me concerning a few sales that I had made through a certain gallery. After thanking him, I told him that while I was always very pleased when people wanted to collect my paintings, I was pretty sure I was losing money after the gallery commissions and discounts were subtracted from the retail price.

Yes, it is always nice to sell your work. It means that somebody wants to live with your art and/or believes that your work will increase in value. To some extent, it means they believe in you as a creative force, the economic value of your work and/or in your personal vision; all of which is something of an honor.

However, if I had continued to sell paintings with the prices and the discounted commission I was receiving from that particular gallery, then I could not afford to continue to make art. I could not afford to continue to live indoors. I do not have the luxury of losing money on sales. I cannot afford this. I have bills to pay, as well as rent, groceries, health care, art supplies, studio expenses and so on. That's the reality. At the time, I had to choose between continuing to lose money on sales and making it on my own. I then chose to sell on my own, and not at less than half of my bottom line. And I have sold my work ever since at a higher frequency than any of my previous galleries ever have.

One cannot afford to live while working full-time at minimum wage and pay all necessary expenses if you are supporting yourself, even in the simplest life (at least not in the U.S.). This is what is meant by a living wage. Not making a living wage characterizes the plight of the working poor. Receiving a living wage means that you can pay for all your basic expenses. Poverty is not a virtue. It is an unhealthy condition. The stress it causes, the time it consumes, the health that poverty leeches from artists results in much less art being produced. Everyone loses.

There is the argument that earning minimum wage or below is better than earning nothing, but at that rate you will soon do without dental and/or health care, good nutrition, shoes without holes, minimally decent housing, and safe, reliable transportation. With being paid minimum wage or below you will not be able to buy art supplies, have a work space and continue moving forward in your creative endeavors.

There are some galleries that expect you to produce and produce and produce. But if the means of production are not being supported, then how are you supposed to continue to produce high-quality work?

Years ago, I was briefly affiliated with another gallery that had asked me to lower the prices on my paintings two hours before the reception of my solo exhibition. During previous group shows at the same gallery, the owner had me setting my own prices with no problem. For this exhibition I had presented them with my price list a few weeks early. The week before the opening the owner's partner informed me that everything was absolutely okay with the list, everything I did was consistent, and we were all set to go. So, when the owner called demanding that I lower my prices at the last minute, I refused. When I showed up at the reception, she was cross with me. I told her that I was already painting for minimum wage, and that I couldn't go any lower. Her immediate response was "all my artists get minimum wage". I ended my relationship with the gallery after this show.

Affordable Art

The term "affordable art", used often and loosely as a selling point, bothers me. What is meant by "affordable"? The definition of the word affordable is; when the cost of goods or services fits within the financial means of the purchaser. It is when something sells for an amount that one can afford to pay.

Then we need to ask, affordable to whom? For one person, $2,000 is a small fortune and not the least bit affordable, especially when there are bills to pay and mouths to feed. For someone else it is petty cash and easily spent without thinking. For a third person $2,000 might be just right for their budget, a sizable investment, but one available to their means.

Everyone has a different sense of economics, even if their financial situations are quite similar. There are well-to-do people who complain about paying $500 for a unique, high-quality piece of art, and there are others who think it is well worth spending $5,000 on something they desire.

Another question to ask; is "affordable art" affordable to the artist to produce? I have yet to see this question brought into the equation during any discussion of affordable art. If you know how much it really costs to create your artwork, then you will know what is affordable to you.

I once saw a call for an "affordable art'" benefit sale for some cause which set a $300 price limit so that the work would then be "affordable". The sponsoring organization took a 50% commission on all sales and there was a $20 entry fee. If a piece of artwork sells at the highest price, then it would go like this: $300 less the 50% commission = $150, less the $20 fee = $130 to cover every cost and expense on the artist's list. EVERY cost and expense. Which might cover things if the piece sold is one of a large print run and the frame was cheap, or was a very small part of a much larger series. Maybe. At this point it becomes a donation.

Years ago, during an open studios event, someone I knew from art school decided that he wanted a particular painting of mine. I had already deeply discounted my prices, being in desperation mode at the time. All he could ask was "Can't you do better by me?" Even though the price was quite low and it was one of my finer paintings from that year. This is someone who I basically liked, and I also knew he could afford to pay the original low price for the painting. He spent a significant amount of money on nice clothes, which was a priority for him, and that's okay. But why should I further undercut the value of my art just so he could get a bargain, especially when he didn't need to make such a request?

Years later, I still have that painting. I have no regrets. It is a unique beauty, and I get to keep it for anyone who shares or visits my home, or it will eventually sell to someone who truly values such a one-of-a-kind piece of fine art.

The term "affordable art" is borderline offensive. In my opinion, it devalues the artist's labor and creativity. It reduces the piece of art to a commodity and not much else, whereas fine art is more than solely the physical object. There is vision, heart and a piece of the artist's soul involved. Affordable art matches the sofa, and usually means cheap, bargain, assembly line, motel motif, and for much of which the word "art" is very loosely applied.

It is also insulting to the low-income population, many of whom may wish to collect art someday, but cannot at this point in time. What does it imply when you can't even afford the affordable art, which probably isn't affordable to someone with limited means. A better term to use is "inexpensive art", although that too, is a somewhat relative term. However, the word "inexpensive" is more clear and expressive of meaning, and less insulting to both the artist and the potential art collector.

If someone says that your work is not affordable, they may truly not be able to afford it. Or they may be saying that your work is not worth it to them, even though they can afford whatever they may want. Don't back down. Your work will eventually sell to someone who will respect it, as well as respect the artist who created it.

Selling Too Low

Over the years, it has often been stated that it is better to sell more work at a lower price, than fewer pieces at a higher price. It has been said it is better to sell two pieces at $300 each, than one at $500. However, what does it really cost to create that work? Is it the $100 for materials quoted, or is there another $150 in overhead per piece? That would leave any leftover balance for the artist's labor at $50. Is $50 sufficient pay for the time involved, or does the artist need $250 to break even for the hours you put into your work? Any time you read one of these articles or posts, and they seem to pop up every now and again, refer to your own calculations for a more realistic view.

Question the initial premise of anything similar you may read. If you are actually making a decent profit, then don't worry about it. But chances are a little more mathematics may be in order. Lose a bit more money with each and every consecutive sale, and you will soon be painting with a barrel for a smock. Not comfortable.

If you are being financially supported, have family money, made wise investment or business decisions when you were younger, or have won the lottery, then selling below cost may not be an issue for you as an individual. However, selling below cost will devalue artwork in general, as well as your own work, and makes it harder for other artists to get a fair price. If you do not need to be paid, then count your blessings, keep your prices in line with the market, and then use the money you don't need from your sales to buy work from other artists. You get to be a collector too. Everyone wins.

A few years back, I attended a bead fair. I'm something of a bead geek, so I know what the general price range should be for both unstrung beads and finished jewelry. I noticed one booth where a woman was selling beaded jewelry for only the cost of the beads and findings. Meanwhile, other beadworkers at the fair were trying to be paid for their labor as well as their materials. This seemed like unfair selling practices to me.

I have often read that is better to sell your artwork cheap, than to have it taking up space. That's not necessarily true. I have had sales turned down in the past because I would not cheapen my art or the way I do business. Okay. No problem. I can wait. Those paintings often sell later on, sometimes within the year, and sometimes for an even higher price, and then to someone who really appreciates the work and honors the artist that created it.

Unlike most things that are for sale, fine craft or artwork will not disintegrate or rot, go out of season, not fit anymore, or go out of style. If it is timeless in technique, is archival, and genuine of spirit then it will last and have value for generations to come. Yes, artwork takes up space, but that's how it goes. All physical things take up space. If you sell cheap now, then people will continue to expect cheapness from you and your work will then take a much longer time to gain value.

The simple reality is that you need to recover your costs; for the supplies, overhead expenses and time spent making your artwork. Simple as that. You are the person who needs to go over your own books and make your own decisions. Art that is sold below cost, expenses and labor equals art that is given away, either partially or completely. If you underprice your work then you are giving away your money and/or your time to make a sale. Ask yourself how long you can afford to continue to do this. If someone tries to guilt you into selling your work for cheap, then remember that in general artists give a lot of time, effort, material, money and large pieces of their souls away FOR FREE on a regular basis. Start taking note of what you already give away. It will most likely be a very interesting and generous list.

Consistency

Consistency in the pricing of artwork is a measure of professionalism for any artist. Your prices cannot be based on passing whims and random pork bellies. Being an artist is too personal a business. It is not just the product you create that interests buyers, but often your reputation and persona are part of the deal. If you want your art to have great value in the eyes of others, then you must behave in a way that demonstrates a high level of value. If you want to be taken seriously, then you must act seriously.

Being Consistent with Your Pricing Structure

By having a consistent price structure, potential collectors will know what to expect, there will be no rude surprises (at least not coming from you), and there will be clear justification for the prices of your work. No buyer will feel cheated, and they will be able to trust you.

Never lower the prices on any body of work that you exhibit. If you lower your prices, you will not grow the value of your work. Hold them steady and slowly raise them over time. Meanwhile, improve the quality of your artwork and actively work on your career. See the chapter on Growth for some ideas on how to do this.

Undercutting previous collectors is bad for your reputation. It is also unethical. It does not bode well for future sales at your regular prices. You will not be trusted to price your artwork fairly in the future. You might lower your prices again at a later date, as there is no record that you won't. Neither you nor your actions will be seen as professional. Once again, if you want to be taken seriously, then act the part.

Lowering your prices is unfair to your previous collectors. Buying art is a major event, both in money and emotional investment. You are not selling electronics or last season's clothing or anything that has been manufactured for the masses. What you create and sell does not have to be cleared out so that you have rack space for this year's model. Fine art and craft is different than the things people buy at the mall or the big box store.

Your prices should be consistent both in and out of the studio. They should be consistent no matter where your work is showing and selling. A $900 drawing will be priced at $900 in the studio, $900 in the gallery, $900 online, and $900 at the outdoor art fair. Commissions may vary, depending on where the drawing is sold. The same drawing will retail for $900, the buyer will pay $900, but the artist may receive a different portion of the sale, depending on where it has sold. This is to be expected. The important thing is that the retail price remains consistent across the board.

When an artist sells work out of the studio it means that the artist can get a decent price for their work, although sometimes they might be passing on a courtesy commission to their gallery or dealer. Depending on the amount of any commission, or if there is none, the artist will sometimes make a little more money with each sale and sometimes a little less, but the artist's pricing structure will be consistent and professional.

The advantages to collectors who buy directly from artists are not in large discounts, but in visiting the studio. There is a personal interaction with the artist, a positive relationship may build and they get to see where and how the artist works (open studios are very popular for this reason). They also get the opportunity to view and purchase works that are not normally on exhibition.

Cheap Art

There is a theory that goes; "the lower your art is priced, the more will sell". This is a myth. It may work okay for a few people, but that depends on what they are selling. If this were generally true, then only discount stores would remain in business and only things on sale would sell. Dented cans and bolts of stained fabric would be flying out the door. Is your artwork imperfect? Is it mass-produced for the masses? Probably not. Don't people often buy new and unique things in excellent condition? Don't they ever pay full-price? Yes, they do.

If you are going to keep lowering your prices to sell more artwork, then where is the break-off point? How low will you go? Where you are paid minimum wage for your skilled labor, or will you go completely unpaid for your time, or even below material costs? Will you in actuality be paying the buyer to take it away? Unless you are holding a going-out-of-business sale, do not set yourself up to go out of business.

If your prices are too low, then the perceived value of both your artwork and your abilities as an artist will be considered inferior. Art created by a working artist that is priced at the hobby or student level is a sign of either desperation or amateur status. People will expect to continue to be able to buy your work at rock-bottom prices for some time to come.

Things priced cheaply are considered cheap. They will not be valued. In the long run, they may not even be cared for. Someone who pays a decent price for a work of art will not fold it up and stuff it into a closet or store it downstairs in the damp basement. They will take care of the artwork, proudly display it, and if for some reason they don't want it anymore, they will most likely sell it or give it to someone who, hopefully, will care for it.

Affordability

With keeping a consistent pricing structure you may wonder how you can continue to sell artwork when the economy slows down. Maybe there are people who are interested in buying your work, but they can't afford it. How do you make sales to collectors who are on a low budget without having to lower your prices?

There are a number of ways for you to have economic growth and still have inexpensive work available for sale. See the chapter on Growth for ideas. The important thing is to hold the prices steady on your current bodies of exhibit-quality work. Do not lower your prices.

If someone genuinely cannot afford my work, I am not offended. In fact, I understand. Buying art is a major purchase. Many people cannot do this on a whim. If someone cannot afford my work, but is sincerely interested in doing so, I try to find something that they can afford, and/or I stay in touch with them. This way, when I develop a new set of studies, or a series of smaller paintings, I give them an early chance to purchase one of these more inexpensive pieces. Plus, their economic situation may improve sooner or later, and they can then afford one of my finished paintings.

However, not being able to afford the price on a piece of artwork and whining about it are two very different things. Whiners are annoying. Show them your calculation charts. Let them know how much hard work and overhead expense goes into your art. Be polite, but direct about it, and they may come around to seeing the value in your work. Sometime people just need to understand why an original painting is worth more than one of those assembly-line sofa-sized mall things. Then they're cool about the situation.

Others will continue to whine for whatever reason. As tempting as it may be to ask them if they would be willing to work for minimum wage themselves, just say that you cannot afford to sell your work at a loss, let alone undercut previous collectors. Period. Do this with dignity. It is possible that one day they will change their tune and return to you with the purchase price in hand.

Selling Out of the Studio

There is the misconception among some that it is standard practice for artists to sell their work for half price from the studio, whether they have gallery representation or not. It is as though the artist's studio is a factory outlet. Considering that most factory outlets these days do not sell things for half price, this is not such an effective analogy. Most outlet stores sell things at a slight discount, and usually for imperfect, overstocked and/or last season's items. Your studio is not a factory outlet. You are not a factory.

Many collectors expect this and some artists discount 50% automatically when selling directly from their studios. This is a terrible practice for a number of reasons. As discussed many times earlier, artists who do this severely devalue their work. It is also very unfair to collectors who pay full price to purchase works from galleries and other exhibition venues. Word will get around and no one will want to buy that artist's work when it is on exhibit. Why should the collector pay retail at a gallery when they can pay half price during a visit to the studio?

Do not do this to your dealer. It is unethical to undercut someone who is trying to help you. You might make an extra sale now, but you will lose so much more in the long run. Your reputation with galleries will be damaged. Many dealers will not want to do business with you.

Galleries fear this situation and some automatically mistrust all their artists, suspecting that we all behave this badly. Mistrustful galleries will not supply artists with the names and mailing addresses of buyers of their work, even if supplying this information is the law in some states. Not knowing who has bought your artwork seriously affects provenance, which is keeping track of who has bought your work.

This can also backfire on the gallery. Let's say that an honest artist does not have a list of their collectors from their gallery. What if someone contacts the artist independently to request a studio visit, and then buys something? How will that artist know to send a courtesy commission to the gallery if they don't know that this collector is a gallery contact? They may have found the artist online, and not mention seeing their work in the gallery from a previous time.

Studio Sales Events

When you have a special sale or partake in an open studios event, you will still need to have consistent prices. These events are more for getting people into your studio so that they can see the breadth of your work, or to introduce a new body of work to the public or to friends. It is not just a 'sales event', unless you are quitting being an artist altogether, in which case it doesn't matter anymore. Clear it out.

We had a moving sale and open house event a number of years ago. The flyer offered some bargains, as well as the last chance to buy our better work at current prices. Since we were moving 1900 miles away, and time would eventually pass, our prices would soon be going up.

One person became offended by having the word "bargains" on the flyer. He misinterpreted what was actually for sale and for how much. Since he had recently bought some drawings from my boyfriend, this was an issue to him. However the only bargains my boyfriend offered during this event were his quick gesture (figure) sketches. The prices on his finished drawings at the open house sale were the exact same as they were when this collector came to look at his work at an earlier date. It took some explaining, but things were eventually straightened out.

Everybody else understood the nature of the beast. My bargains were the three following things: much earlier student work, some old assemblage experiments and a few cloud studies on canvas board. Our current bodies of work stayed at their regular prices. A few of the bargains, as well as some finished works at their regular prices, sold for each of us.

We also sold half-used supplies, tools, studio furniture, art books, frames and still-life props. These were the real bargains. It was like a garage sale for other creative types. One person spent $1.25 on a tiny bag of beads and another spent $2500 on a pair of small oil paintings. This is a good way to clean out your studio and make some quick cash at the same time. Invite all your artist friends and associates. Tell them to bring their friends and associates.

What to do with Artwork that Just Needs to Go

For whatever reason, you may want or need to clear out work that isn't selling. In that case, this is the art to donate to good causes, barter for worthwhile things, or roll-up if possible and more easily store.

There are ways to sustain the value of this work while letting it go. You can donate pieces to worthy causes. See the chapter on Giving It Away concerning donations. Be careful of donating too much in any one year. Also be aware that donated work will reflect on your reputation. People will be seeing it at auction, in a benefit exhibit or hanging on the wall of a beneficiary. And your name will be attached. Unless the date of creation is clearly posted, people may think it is your latest work. Eek!

On the other hand, let's say you just have way too much older artwork cluttering up your studio, work that you will never try to show or sell again. And there is a wonderful local organization or shelter that could use something interesting and/or inspiring on their walls. Consider donating multiple pieces as a group. You can always insist that there is a date attached, a little plaque with an explanation of this being much earlier work, or it can hang as anonymous art.

You can give artwork away to family and friends as gifts. Your art will still keep its worth, because many people do give valuable things to the people they care about. If you treasure someone, then price is no object. Bestowing something valuable upon them does not decrease the value of the gift, not in the least. Of course, you will have to consider whether or not they may appreciate something that is cumbersome or so unwanted by you.

If storage is the issue, then paintings on canvas can be removed from the frames and rolled up. Other work might be able to be taken apart carefully. However, dismantling artwork could cause irreparable damage. Do your research first. There are often many options for storing artwork, and if you can't think of any, then ask your artist friends to brainstorm for ideas with you. You can also get ideas from home improvement stores, as well as books and websites. Wander the aisles with an open mind. Do some research on storage solutions.

Artwork that just has to go can also be used as bonus giveaways. When I lived in California there was a couple that bought six paintings from me in a period of two years. The sixth sale was made soon before I moved away. I had two medium-sized, very heavy mixed-media-on-plywood paintings. I offered the woman (who made the last sale by herself) one of the two heavy paintings as a gift of gratitude for buying so much of my work in such a short period of time. She was thrilled. My albatross became her treasure.

If a collector buys a certain number of pieces during a determined time period or spends a certain amount of money on your work all at once, then consider offering free artwork as a bonus, incentive or thank you. They get a freebie from this pile, or they can choose something at no extra cost from that stack over there. Be clear about which work is available as bonus giveaways, and that all of your other work is available for regular sale only.

You can barter your artwork for goods or services that have the same monetary value. Bartering can keep the value up as long as the trade is equal. This will only work for you as long as the goods and/or services are something you can really use or need, or it is for something that you truly want.

Another idea to consider is if someone wants to buy a $2000 piece of art, but they can only afford $750. If you really want them to have that particular piece of art, then barter the amount of the difference to keep the value up. Again, this will only work if they have something or a service to offer you that is worth $1250, or whatever the balance may be.

Holding Steady

Unsold work of good quality will often sell, although it may take awhile. I have had people buy paintings that were freshly varnished, as well as paintings that were over ten years old.

People will pay good money, and at times lots of it, for the things that they value. Most collectors will not care what year a piece of artwork was created if they really want to buy it. Hold on.

Keeping your prices stable is an option in any economy. You don't have to raise the prices on your good work. But you don't have to lower them either. Many newer collectors will appreciate the fact that you are aware and concerned enough to hold steady for the time being.

Consistency in Discounting

Like having a consistent pricing structure for your work, have a consistent discount policy for when you sell out of studio or through your own website. Once this policy is set, keep it steady for years at a time.

The standard discount is 10%, given only to reward repeat collectors and/or people who buy two or more pieces of artwork at one time. Another option is "buy two paintings at once and receive a small credit towards a future sale". Sometimes covering the costs of shipping is offered in lieu of a discount.

Sales Commissions

As the word "commission" relates to the visual arts, there are two commonly used meanings. One definition covers work that the artist is paid by somebody to do, as in a portrait commission, a public art project, or maybe illustrations for a book. As a verb this means being commissioned to create a work of art. As a noun it is like a job, as in a commission to do a portrait. It could also be used as an adjective such as a commissioned mural.

The definition being discussed in this chapter concerns sales commissions. This is the percentage of the retail price of a piece of artwork that is paid (usually as a percentage automatically removed from your check) to the gallery, dealer, agent, exhibiting venue or sponsoring organization. This is called a sales commission. It is also a job definition in a way, because you are commissioning a person, place or organization to sell your art for you. In turn, you pay them a percentage of the sales price to do this work on your behalf.

For example, you are exhibiting work at Gallery A this month. One of your drawings sells for a retail price of $1,000. Gallery A takes a 40% commission. If the price of your drawing is $1,000 and the gallery gets a 40% commission of that price, then they receive $400 for their efforts in selling your work. As the artist, you get $600. It is a 60/40 split.

Calculating Sales Commissions

When you calculate your prices, remember that the basic cost of producing your artwork does not include any sales commissions. In an ideal world the total cost of creating your art, per piece, would be less than 50% of retail, so that the gallery portion does not come out of your pocket when the commission is set at 50%.

In my experience, I have paid commissions of 20%, 30%, 33%, 40% and 50%. Anything below 40%, and the exhibition was probably not held at a commercial gallery, but at an independent, non-commercial venue. Museums, community art centers and other non-commercial exhibition venues usually ask for commissions at or below 40%.

Galleries are different. Artist friends of mine remember the olden days of the 1960s and 70s when the gallery standard for a sales commission was between 30% and 35%, with a few stretching it to 40%. This was for total representation within a limited area, maybe a city or a small region (such as within a 50-mile circumference of the gallery). The gallery did everything a professional gallery should, with the artist being paid between 60% and 70% of retail. By the early 1990s only a handful of galleries remained with their commissions set at 40%. At this point most galleries were taking a full 50% commission.

Figuring the monetary value of a percentage is simple. Take your original number and multiply it by the percentage amount with a decimal point in front. For example, what is 40% of $360? Multiply $360 by .40 (that's point forty) to get your answer: 360 x .40 = 144. Therefore, 40% of $360 is $144. Easy!

Never state a wholesale price when setting prices, always retail. For example: Gallery B takes a 50% commission. You are consigning a $2,000 painting in an exhibit. If it sells, then the gallery gets $1,000 and you get $1,000. Meanwhile, Gallery C, in another city, wants you to state your wholesale price when you leave the painting with them. If you agree to $1,000 as a wholesale price, then they can turn around and sell your painting for $3,000. You get $1,000, but they get $2,000, which is a 33.3% vs. 66.7% split. This is not fair for either the artist or the collector.

Non-Gallery Commissions

Simple consignment arrangements and juried shows are obviously different than gallery representation. When it comes to sales commissions at these venues, realize that individual long-term promotion is not involved.

Offices, stores and restaurants sometimes will take nothing, or a commission as low as 10–20%, but usually not much more. They benefit from having original art hanging on their walls. By holding informal exhibitions they can avoid paying rental fees for having the artwork. It becomes more of an exchange in services. Sales of art are usually slow at these types of venues. However, you never know, you might get lucky, and the experience can be valuable for an artist in the early stages of their career.

Juried shows that are held in public venues such as college galleries, municipal galleries, libraries, city hall corridors and so on have a range of commissions from zero to maybe 30%. They have some of the same expenses as galleries do, but they often have other revenue streams supporting public exhibitions of artwork.

Commissions for juried exhibitions at museums and art centers are often set between 20 and 40%.

Juried exhibitions that are held in galleries usually match the regular percentage charged to the gallery stable artists. The main argument for this is that if the regular artists in the gallery stable pay 40 or 50%, then so should everyone else.

There are two ways to look at this. Outside (non-represented) artists get the benefit of the gallery reputation partially built by the regular artists. On the other hand, artists only showing once on consignment in a juried show do not get all the benefits of personal long-term representation.

It's a mixed bag and I lean towards not paying as much, maybe five or ten percent less, because of there being no personal representation. On occasion I may still enter these 50% commission juried shows at galleries. I'm not thrilled with the commission being that high, but at times the career opportunity seems to be worth it.

Paying Commissions on Framing

Most venues expect paintings, watercolors, pastels, photographs, prints and drawings to be framed, with the artist carrying the full expense. They consider it to be part of the deal, like the cost of varnishing a painting. Paintings on thick supports are sometimes the rare exception. Occasionally a gallery will help with framing costs. However, it is written into many contracts that the artist is 100% responsible for this. Still, the gallery gets reimbursed for 50% of the cost of the framing if the piece sells, even if they didn't pay anything for the frame.

I have read advice saying that artists should never pay a commission on frames. Either the gallery should pay 50% of the cost of framing or they should take a commission on the price of the artwork minus the frames. For example, a $700 framed lithograph minus $100 for the frame equals $600 that will be split for the commission. At 50% this equals $300 each. In actuality I have never seen this done. More likely, the $700 price will be split 50/50, with the artist getting $350. Subtract $100 for the cost of the frame, and that leaves the artist with $250 for the lithograph. The gallery still gets their $350.

There are two ways to look at this issue. If the gallery insists on expensive frames, or springs the idea on you at the last minute so that you cannot plan for the expense, then I think they should reimburse you their 50% share for the cost of framing. It also depends if the frame is really a part of the artwork or not, or is simply a device for presentation.

The frames that I often use are sized for small paintings and are relatively inexpensive, being unfinished wood. However, I put in hours of my time and employ other materials in finishing them. Therefore, they end up costing me at least $100 each in materials and labor. I see the frames as both an integral part of my art since I paint on panel (my paintings cannot be self-framed), and as another expense I have to lay out so that the work is presentable and ready to hang. I pay 100% for my frames both in money and time, and when a commission is paid on a sale, I am out whatever that percentage is, as it relates to the frame. But I can see how it should be included as part of the piece, too.

However, no place I have ever encountered, or seen in years and years of listings, has ever offered to take their commission on the price of the work minus the expense of framing. Always include the cost and time of framing your work into your overhead costs and labor. Even if you don't make or finish the frames yourself, there is still time involved with ordering, measuring sizes, and so on.

Paying Commissions to Galleries

This is not a book about gallery relationships, but about pricing, so I will only go ankle deep into the subject of galleries. However, paying commissions is a major part of your financial relationship with a gallery, and it will affect your pricing structure.

Standard gallery commission these days is 50%, with a few charging 40%. However, there are now some galleries that take a 60% cut, with the artist getting only 40% of the retail price. And the artists are the ones creating the art! I think this is outrageous. Plus, some venues are now asking artists to pay for all or part of the promotional expenses and/or the costs of the reception, invitations, etc. There are small galleries with stables consisting of dozens and dozens of artists that insist on large geographical areas of exclusive representation. Only blue chip galleries should demand exclusivity in a whole state or region since it seems only they concentrate major resources on their artists. Some places even rent out wall space and take a large commission or an up-front fee, but that is a different type of gallery all together, one best to be avoided.

Never agree to pay a commission of more than 50%. Galleries can only get away with higher commissions if enough artists are willing to let them. Truthfully, galleries cannot do without artists, but artists can do without galleries. I still think there are many reasons for galleries to exist and I would hate to see them disappear. I believe there are still many galleries out there that have honorable business practices and have the experience to do well for their artists, but they are getting fewer and farther between, which is unfortunate for all of us.

Go over your price list with the gallery or other venue well in advance of any exhibition. Have them sign off on an agreement with you, and keep a copy with their signature in your own files. On two occasions I have been asked to change my prices on the day of the reception, when verbal agreements were made well in advance. It is as though they don't have faith in the value of the work, or in their own ability to sell artwork at a price that is reasonable to both the artist and potential collectors. To have to deal with these conflicts on the day of your reception when you need to appear confident and happy is not a good thing.

Another thing to consider are secondary commissions, sometimes called split commissions. Sometimes, especially with a gallery relationship, either you, your gallery or a third party organizes an exhibition of your work at another venue. Often in this situation, the retail price of the artwork gets split three ways. When this happens, make sure that you always get your 50% no matter what. Your equation does not change. The labor, cost, and overhead that go into your work remain the same. The other parties do less selling, and share their labor, cost, and overhead, therefore they should split the difference. How that 50% is divided is up to them. This is how it should be, but not always is. Sometimes, artists are told to take a cut in their percentage as well. Be aware of this.

I do not want to be criticizing solely galleries, juried shows, collectors, etc. I cannot stress enough how important it is for us artists to live up to our end of the bargain. Too many artists conduct themselves in the manner of the unreliable, flaky stereotype. The more professional we behave, both individually and as a group, the better we will be treated in the long run. In order to demand respect from others, we must show respect for ourselves by our actions. And when someone treats us right, we should always let him or her know how much we appreciate it.

Meanwhile, a cross-section of people in the art world from artists to conscientious dealers and curators have observed that overall, things seem to be growing more and more difficult for artists. Too many galleries, dealers and exhibition venues become greedier every year. Commission percentages go up, jury and entry fees go up, new fees are introduced, artists are expected to pay more of the costs of exhibition and promotion, and to pay shipping in both directions, not just to the venue. A three-person show is now sometimes considered a solo exhibition, when two artists showing together has been the status quo for a few decades. Once upon a time were there ever real solo exhibitions with only one artist showing?

Galleries and Discounts

Many galleries have a discount policy. It used to be that artwork might be discounted for multiple sales of one artist's work to the same collector, often at the same time. Sometimes a discount might be given to a museum interested in collecting an artist's work. These discounts were only offered as an incentive, and/or to reward a collector's continuing interest in and support of a particular artist. This discount was usually 10%, although a museum might receive more. Galleries would then absorb the discount out of their share of the commission. With repeat collectors and museum collections, the artist would become more valuable to the gallery and to future collectors. Prices could soon be raised. Everyone benefits. The artist would still receive their originally agreed-upon share for any sales.

The standard right now is still 10%, but most galleries often insist on splitting the discount with the artist. It used to be there was a reason for offering a discount to a collector, but there are some galleries where it is now automatic with any sale, just to move the work out the door. One gallery did this with four pieces I had on consignment with them (I was not represented by them and had no long-term career advantage). Because of their easy discounting policy I received 45% of the retail price for my work. Four different buyers in four different states on four different days received the ten percent discount. One set of collectors even bragged about it in front of me, like I was supposed to be happy. As it was, I was still nowhere near covering my costs with the full 50% commission.

This is how it works. A $2,000 painting discounted at 10% sells for $1,800. Your 50% share is now $900, not the original $1,000. You are losing 5% percent of retail, by splitting the discount with the gallery, but you are really losing 10% of your 50% payment, since 10% of 50% equals 5% of the total. You are down $100, which is 10% of $1,000.

Think about what this does to the value of your work, or your own consistent pricing structure and discount policy. Is this a game that the gallery and purchaser play with each other, but with the artist paying the price? There used to be reasons for discounting artwork besides hastening a sale. In my opinion, someone who really wants to buy the painting will pay either $2,000 or $1,800. Someone who can afford $1,800 can also afford $2,000. But that $100 difference in commission can mean a lot to an individual artist.

Always ask the gallery about their discount policy before setting prices for any consigned work. Ask what the percentage is and under what circumstances the discount is offered or given to a collector. If you don't agree with their policy you may be able to work out a compromise. If not, then at least you will know ahead of time what will be expected of you. It may be unpleasant, but it won't be a surprise.

Commissions on Studio Sales

Another issue concerns studio sales and passing on commissions to galleries or dealers. This only pertains to the artist being represented by a gallery or a dealer and the sale qualifies for a commission, because of location and/or relationship. The standard is 20%, or once was and still should be. I have heard of galleries charging up to 50% for a courtesy commission. In most other businesses such commissions are lower. They are in general. The fine arts have some of the highest commissions as a percentage paid to the agent or seller.

There are many shades of gray and all kinds of variables when it comes to paying commissions on studio sales. Some things to be considered are:

1. Is the representing gallery sending the collector to the artist's studio to buy work?
2. Is the artist represented by a gallery, but still has studio sales with collectors from the artist's past or their own personal circles?
3. Does the artist have work on consignment with the gallery (although not contracted nor part of the gallery stable) and is the artist hosting a studio visit with a collector from the gallery?
4. What about sales from the artist's own website?
5. What about sales commissions on portrait commissions and other commissioned work, independent of the gallery?
6. What happens when the gallery sends a client to a non-commercial exhibition, such as a museum benefit, where the artist may already be paying a commission on any sales?

On the other hand, what if an artist sends their own clients to the gallery, introducing their own past collectors to the gallery. What if these collectors then buy the work of other artists from that gallery? How does the first artist financially benefit from this situation, which the gallery then benefits from?

What galleries do for their percentage

The best galleries have a right to ask for a 50% commission on the sale of your work for representing you. If they hold up their end of the bargain, they have plenty of work to do and a definite set of expenses. A professional gallery provides a minimum of the following for their percentage on the sales of your work. These are the services you are paying for with a 50% commission:

You should expect to have one solo exhibition at least every other year, and to be included in one group exhibit at the gallery once a year, minimum. You should have a continuing presence in the back room, and the gallery staff should be constantly showing your work to their clientele. A professional gallery covers all costs of promotion, publicity, marketing, advertising, invitations, receptions, insurance, and the burden of loss if a client defaults on any payments. They will get you reviews and previews, and your work will have a presence on the gallery website. This has been the standard for decades (except for the website, obviously). They will establish a relationship of trust and open communication with you.

The best not only will promote your work through their gallery, but they will also help to advance your career. This is good for both you and the gallery. An artist who has a presence in museums, in touring exhibitions, art expositions and other prestigious non-commercial exhibits, is a positive reflection on the gallery. A good gallery will work with you to expand your career in these venues, through exhibitions and collections. When one artist does well, then all the other artists represented by the gallery benefit through the exposure.

If they do any less, then their percentage should be less. You do a ton of work, they should do an equal ton of work. It should be an evenly balanced, mutually beneficial arrangement.

Like you, gallery owners have many other expenses and significant overhead in running their business. They have employees to pay, rent or mortgage, office supplies, postage, utilities, cleaning, insurance and association fees, among many other things. They have to keep up the appearance of an attractive gallery, such as lighting, furnishings, repainting the walls between shows and so on. They have to promote the gallery in general, not just each individual artist. This general promotion will help to sell your art when it is in the back room or in a group show.

You should do your part and behave as professionally as possible. Be responsible, establish excellent communications and always work to deserve their trust. You should supply all your own basic marketing materials such as resume, statement, high-quality images, etc. Do everything in a timely manner. Offer them your best work and make sure that it is always dry and well presented.

They take risks and you take risks, all things being equal. A good, top notch, excellent gallery works hard for and deserves their 50% commission, but not any more than that.

In Conclusion on Commissions

There are many talented and truly original artists who cannot afford a gallery relationship because of losses incurred. If you are one of them, you will have to ask yourself if these are long or short-term losses, and is there a future to this relationship where the temporary loss will soon be replaced by gains?

Unless the retail prices on your artwork are double the cost of creating that work (i.e. if your cost is 50% of retail), then the more art you sell, the more money you will lose with each sale. This might be acceptable for a year or two as long as you have some other income. It is also only acceptable in the short run if the gallery is clear with you about your future growth in sales, raised prices, career growth, etc. It is never acceptable for the long run.

Remember, if you have to spend time and energy working for any outside income (such as a day job), then you will not be able to create as much art. You will therefore have less artwork to offer to the gallery or for growing your career. If you are financially supported in any way and don't have to limit the time you spend creating artwork, consider yourself very fortunate.

Raising Prices

Intangible factors such as originality, technical skill, and career level will affect your ability to raise prices. If you want your prices to go up, you will have to grow as an artist, both in your artwork and in your career. You will need to consistently better your art with skill, vision, originality, presentation and so on. You will have to move forward in your career with such things as exhibitions, publications, teaching, residencies and awards. See the chapters on growth and variables for more.

And of course, the market plays a role, as does the economy.

About Raising the Prices on Your Art

You do not need to achieve great leaps and bounds each year. Simply add a few new things to your resume annually. It adds up. Proof of longevity in your career increases the perception of your seriousness as an artist. It is not just the passing of time that is notable, but what you are doing with that time while it is passing. Meanwhile, give more attention to your artwork. Give each piece more of the skill and vision that you have gained over the years. Your work will become more valuable as a result.

Personal growth, growth in your artwork, and to some extent, growth in your career is under your control. Of course, there are rejections and disappointments along the way. They happen to everybody. But there really are good opportunities for artists if you just go looking for them. If things are feeling slow to you, then simply hold your prices steady for the time being. You will eventually sell again, and the level of sales will grow as long as the quality of your work is high and continues to get better. That, plus, you have to get out there. These things are up to you.

Fairness in raising your prices brings not only fairness to the art market in general, but also fairness to yourself and your collectors. Raising your prices slowly and steadily will eventually get you to a point where the cost of sales commissions will be covered and then surpassed. If you are not already there, remember that you have a right to get there, to expect this equalization of things, although you have to do your part too. Raise your prices with reason, with the comparative marketplace, and with the quality of your work all being considered.

Perceived Value

If you raise the price of an item, you will raise the perceived value of that item. There are people who actually prefer paying higher prices for things. A high price tag can signify a quality item. Much of value is perception. People will pay good money, and at times plenty of it, for things that they value. Look at anything in the marketplace. Anything. There is such a wide range of prices out there. And most of it sells or they wouldn't bother making more of the same, including the expensive versions of whatever it is.

Not only wealthy people buy expensive things. Do you always buy the cheapest possible thing? Almost everyone pays a little (or a lot) more for things they really want, or a preferable version of something they need. For example, would you prefer to buy the cheapest, flimsiest serving spoon available from the dollar store or the one that looks a little nicer, and feels better in the hand, from the kitchen store?

There have been many reported cases where prices on artwork have been raised and then the pieces finally sell. Raise the price on a piece of artwork and it will seem more valuable and more desirable. I sometimes think this sort of thing is a dance between collectors, dealers and artists. Any and all parties involved need to agree on some level (even unspoken) that the work is worth it. Perceived value comes from both individual and collective perception. What you think your work is worth, not just in financial terms, but also in critical terms, matters. This is balanced by what your collectors and others perceive your work to be worth, which is then backed by the cold hard numerical facts of previous sales. If you have been selling your work at $2,000 per piece for the last year or so, then you know the market will continue to pay at least that much, if not more, for similar work.

It's relative. A $3,000 painting raised 25% to $4,000 still costs much less than another painting at $7,500. Is one painting more valuable than the other? We would have to see the actual work to decide that. But either way, with raising the price of the first painting to $4,000 it would still be priced a lot lower than the other painting is at $7,500.

If there is a perception that a piece of artwork is underpriced, people may think that there is something wrong with it, that it is not considered valuable enough to be priced well in comparison with the market. If an artist is self-devaluing, meaning they don't value their own work, then why should a collector value it as anything other than a bargain or a steal.

Overpriced Artwork

However, if an artist overprices their work in comparison to its quality, the artist will appear foolish and self-deluded. Overpriced stuff is just overpriced stuff. But even then, a few people will love it just the same and not care. You could try overpricing your work, but that could cause serious problems down the line. Tread very carefully into this territory. If an artist's work is priced retail at more than twice the cost of creating it and the work is seriously lacking in skill and originality, and they haven't had much of a career (especially in the comparative marketplace), then it is overpriced.

High-priced and overpriced are two different things. A high-priced item can also be well priced for what it is. A piece of artwork can be priced at many times the artist's cost if the skill, originality and career factors are all there. Again, see the chapter called Variables.

Maybe you've realized that your work has been overpriced, especially considering the intangible factors. Possibly, you got caught up in some kind of economic bubble or you were marketed as a novelty artist, but now you want to be taken seriously. Maybe you started out pricing your work too high and there were too few sales because you were way out of your league in comparison with similar artists. Meanwhile, you don't want to anger anybody with dumping artwork on the market by slashing prices, which could also do some serious damage to the perceived value of your work in the long run. If any of these cases are true for you, then hold steady and bring your career and artistic abilities in line with your prices, even if it takes a few years to do so. At the very most, undo your overpricing by a small amount, such as 10%. Make it subtle.

How to Raise Your Prices

Raising prices on a steady basis is very reasonable as long as the quality of your work remains consistent, or preferably, improves. Do not become sloppy or lazy because your work is selling. I have observed some artists' prices going up each year while the quality of their work went down. People will notice this. Generally speaking, five to ten percent a year is not a shock to the market.

On occasion, you can go a bit higher than that. With a slow but steady rise in prices, the artwork will continue to sell. Especially if you are not making any money and you hardly have any sales and you know your work is good, this last point having been confirmed by other, more objective people outside yourself. What do you have to lose? If you cannot go any further down, then you may as well start going up.

Raise your prices realistically, fairly and with caution. With consistently improving your artwork and by making a few solid career moves, you can expect the price of your work to go up. If it seems the current market for your work will not support a raise, then hold steady for six months to a year at a time.

Go over all your calculations. Are you meeting your costs? That is your first goal. After that, you want your costs equaling 50% of retail. In other words, the retail price of your artwork should be double the cost of creating it (to cover any sales commissions up to 50%). Next, check all the intangible issues as they relate to your artwork and career. Slowly and steadily raise your prices from there based on these factors.

This is what you are aiming for in 3 steps:

1. Having the cost of creating your artwork meet the retail price, so that by selling directly to your own collectors (without a commission) you do not lose money.

2. Having the cost of creating your artwork meet 50% of the retail price, so that by selling with any commission up to 50% you do not lose money.

3. Having the cost of creating your artwork be less than 50% of retail, so that by selling with any commission up to, and including, 50% you can make a profit.

Profit should not be a dirty word for artists. Profits mean savings, a cushion for when things are lean so that the artist may continue to live and ride out the slow times. With profits, you would be able to invest more in your career, such as covering the costs of shipping your work to distant exhibition venues. It means new materials and equipment for creating your art, money for emergencies, and maybe even a little something nice for all your years of hard work and dedication.

Your Price List

Set a price list for your complete inventory of artwork that is for sale, retail of course, never wholesale. Print it out so that you have a hard copy. Put a deadline on your printed price list stating "Prices good through December 31, 2015", or whatever date makes sense for you, depending on when you are reading this. You may feel better splitting the year in half by writing "Prices good through June 30, 2015". Then evaluate your sales in late June before raising your prices and setting a new end-of-year deadline. Maybe raise your prices five percent for each six-month period, which would equal 10% annually. Hold all your prices steady during any printed time period. Have your price list mean something. Stick to it. Only raise your prices when the deadline is past. Never lower your prices.

You don't have to raise your prices this year, or any other year. If your sales are consistent, you are comfortable with your prices, you are not losing money and you want to hold things steady, then that's okay. It is also perfectly fine when evaluating your price list near the end of any time period to raise the prices on some pieces and to keep others where they are for another six months to a year. That's up to you.

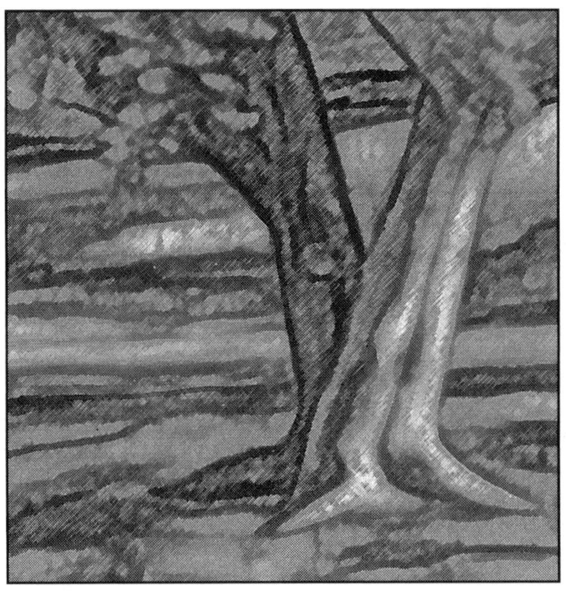

Growth

Growth is integral to raising the value of your artwork, as well as to being an artist. This is the sort of healthy growth that you can achieve as you pass through time. Four things will be discussed in this chapter in no particular order as they pertain to pricing; career growth, growth despite the economy, business growth and artistic growth.

Growth in Your Career

Moving forward with your career is one important way to increase the value of your artwork. Professional accomplishments are the basic items listed on an artist's resume. These include solo and group exhibitions, awards and grants, education, workshops and residencies attended, teaching, lectures and presentations given, having your work in public and private collections, published articles, reviews and getting your artwork in print.

If you are in the early stages of your career, then look into getting your work exhibited in cafés, libraries, and other public places around town. Many non-gallery spaces exhibit artwork. Think about unusual places to show, businesses that compliment your subject matter, or interior design stores where people can see your art in a home setting. Host an open studio or a salon with some of your artist friends and invite everyone that you know and everyone that they know. If you work with interesting subject matter, materials or methods, look into being featured in a local newspaper or a special interest periodical related to your specialty. This is called niche marketing. Having these ideas turn into actualities makes for resume building.

To continue showing your work, apply to juried shows and other calls for entries. Start by showing in your own city, county or region. It takes a while to build recognition. To find listings for exhibition opportunities, look at any local or regional art papers and websites, and regional or national magazines, online or in print, which are geared towards artists (not marketed to collectors, those are different). Contact your local county, regional and/or state art councils. There are also web listings and online newsletters that list many kinds of artists' opportunities.

If you are already years into your career, just continue to do more of the same. Try to add at least a few new entries to your resume annually. After awhile, you will have quite a few accomplishments listed.

Meanwhile, rejections will happen. They happen to everybody. There are usually reasons, both positive and negative. Rejections don't always mean that you aren't good enough. Sometimes, too many qualified applicants submitted work at once. Sometimes, the judging is completely arbitrary. Sometimes, it is all about which artwork looks good together as a complete exhibition, and although the piece you sent in was amazing, it just didn't go with everything else. Sometimes, the juror has ego problems and won't choose anyone who does better work than they do.

Step outside yourself, be objective and evaluate the situation clearly. Does your work need to improve? Does your presentation or the quality of your images need to improve? Do the things you apply for need to improve? Aim higher. It's possible that you might be over-qualified for the sort of thing you are applying for. Ask yourself if are you following all the application instructions correctly. Are you clear about the exhibition theme, if there is one?

Try to see the exhibitions that would not have you (not necessarily at the reception, but during another time). Compare what you submitted to the work that was accepted. Keep a clear mind and be as objective as possible. What you see will often tell you what the story is. If you have been rejected from a number of shows, are there any obvious patterns? If one direction is not working for you, then try another. Someone once told me that opportunities are like buses. Miss one, and another will soon come along.

There really are no career setbacks for artists, although there are certainly lulls. You cannot undo having had a solo show last year. If your drawing was on the cover of an exhibition catalog the summer before last, well, that's a done deal too. If in the midst of all this glory a critic wrote you a bad review in the Sunday paper, let it blow over, and don't include reprints of the article in your promotional packet or on your website (but keep a copy for your own records). Your only two choices are to move forward or stay exactly where you are. You cannot go backwards, even if it genuinely feels that way at times.

You may have some limitations, whether they are physical, family-oriented, financial or logistical. Many issues are only temporary and others can be worked around. If one path is blocked it might mean that you need to take another path. Paths are only limited by your frustration. And they are revealed to you by your imagination.

Growth Despite the Economy

The current economy is a whole different story from anything we've seen for a long time. From when I wrote the first edition of this book in 2002–03, what seemed to be a simple economic downturn has since evolved into the Great Recession. Chances are, you are a part of the 99% and the outside economy is having its way with you and yours to some degree or another.

Just the same, people are still buying art. Artwork is still being sold and commissioned. Private lessons are being given, classes are being filled, exhibitions are being held and many are very well attended. Art is still a priority for many.

Money is still being earned and money is still being spent. Stress that your work has high value per dollar. It won't go out of style, and it will be around for generations to enjoy (as long as it is well-made and archival). Meanwhile, stay in touch with all of your potential collectors, so they won't forget you when things improve financially for them.

Growth in Business

How can you continue to sell work when the economy goes down? Maybe there are people who are interested in buying your work, but they can't afford it. How do you make sales to collectors who are on a tight budget without having to lower your prices? It's not a problem. With a little time and effort, solutions can be created. There are a number of ways for you to have personal economic growth and still have inexpensive work available for sale. The important thing is to hold the prices steady on your current and best bodies of work. Do not lower those prices.

As a painter who has at least three bodies of high-quality and time-intensive work in which I cannot lower my prices, I still have options. From time to time, I work on studies to sharpen my skills. Whenever I do a study, I try to use the best and most archival materials possible, so that the piece may someday be salable. The difference between a study and a finished painting is the amount of time I spend on the actual piece, and the final quality of the picture itself. I also have a number of much earlier paintings and some experimental mixed-media assemblage pieces that I created for specific installations. I have all three of these groups for sale at very low prices; the current studies, the much earlier work and the assemblage pieces. On two separate occasions, I have sold half-finished paintings for about half what the final prices might be. These were paintings that I knew I would never complete. The buyers were both made aware of the unfinished state, but they loved the paintings just the way they were. They were happy. I was happy.

Any student work, sketches, maquettes, material experiments, color studies, samples and so on, can be sold at prices significantly lower than your main bodies of work. You have your regularly priced finished work and you have your "bargain" work. Just don't confuse the two when you are ready to put the work up for sale. Keep them distinct.

This is considered good business practice in general; having a range of prices on your various goods, so that there is something for everyone.

When going through your earlier work and deciding what to sell, remember that some of your older pieces may have value to you, historically-speaking. It's a good idea to keep a few of your favorite examples from each period or body of work. You will then have something to show for a retrospective, keep for your own posterity and to have a personal record of your growth as an artist over the years.

You can easily create different bodies of work specifically for different price ranges. If you are a sculptor who does grand figures in clay, one possibility is to create a series of functional bowls with your own signature touch. Plus, it might be fun to work at the wheel now and then. Anything you do large can also be done smaller. You do not have to look at this as working for the marketplace, but as a chance to experiment on a smaller scale. For example, awhile back I did a series of cloud studies to improve my painting. It was only afterwards that I sold a few of them. The main objective was to "improve my painting". The secondary benefit was that I had something to sell to a person on a tight budget who wanted to buy some of my work.

For artists there is always something new to try, and these explorations can be made so that they are also available for sale. A weaver who creates large tapestries may want to experiment with new materials or color combinations and may not want to invest the time in a big piece. This weaver could do a series of smaller pieces to work out new ideas. Someone who creates stained glass windows may want to experiment in three-dimensions. Instead of creating a full window, a series of small hanging ornaments might be just the thing to learn about all the possibilities.

Think about what you do now and what you might like to explore, either in your own medium or in another one that you find intriguing. This new body of experimental work can be sold at prices lower than your regular body of work. More importantly, think of all the new things you will learn and all the new skills you will acquire in the process. Everybody wins.

Another possibility for having a separate series of lower-priced items to sell is reproductions. This works best for two-dimensional art, but with some creativity this can be applied to three-dimensional work as well. I imagine that manufacturing would be involved with reproducing three-dimensional pieces. I would recommend doing some research and asking the advice of others who have done the same.

Two-dimensional reproductions are not to be confused with prints, which are one-at-a-time hand-pulled etchings, lithographs, monotypes and such. Reproductions are machine-made, although the original settings need the human touch. Some reproductions are best created in limited runs, like glicées. This creates more value for each piece. Other items, like postcards and full-sized posters may be unlimited. Always let your customer know which is which, and stick to it. Again, consistency is important. Do not sell a limited run of fifty glicées, and then decide to run another fifty, thereby devaluing the first group. The purchasers of the original run will never trust you again. However, done with integrity and style, fine art reproductions are a wonderful way to have a relatively inexpensive line of work.

You could think about creating products bearing your images, as opposed to fine art reproductions. Some common ideas are magnets, coffee mugs, t-shirts, puzzles, and the list goes on and on. This sort of things works best with a niche market, such as dog images geared towards dog people. You will have to decide for yourself if this is palatable to you or not. It might be selling out or it might be a tool for supporting and publicizing the other work that you do. Going this route could get your images and your name out there and the financial rewards might support more serious artwork. Or maybe not. Either way, it would create a lower-priced body of work. However, similar to having reproductions made, there would be the issues of capital, manufacturing, storage and marketing to consider.

There is also the licensing of your images and designs, but that is a whole other world that I could not begin to discuss here. Just hold on tight to your copyrights and be careful of what you sign. Research licensing the same way you might research the printing or manufacturing of reproductions.

Time-payments are another way to make your artwork more available to those who cannot pay you all at once. For some people it is easier to make payments over time, than to come up with the money to buy something right away.

I have had a few time-payment arrangements that worked out very well for both the collector and myself. However, in the distant past, I have also had two situations that didn't end so well because I trusted so-called friends to finish paying me after they each had the paintings in hand. Both times, I was stiffed on the final payments.

The protocol for time-payments for purchasing artwork is for the artist to keep the piece until the final payment is made. A contract should be written which includes the dates and the exact (or minimum) amount of each payment. Include conditions for late payments, defaults on payments, and if minds are allowed to be changed concerning the sale. Commit that the artwork will be kept safe and in excellent condition until the final payment is made, when ownership of the piece is handed over to the buyer. Make sure that both you and the collector are in agreement and feel secure about the details of the arrangement. I highly recommend that you research legal issues and contracting for artists if you decide to go this route for a sale.

I have studied a fair bit about the nature of money. As a self-supporting artist, I am always trying to crack this nut. One thing I have learned is the importance of having multiple sources of income. This is actually a pretty common idea for people who have a higher comfort level with the idea of money (which, by the way, you are clearly open to since you are reading this book). What is meant by multiple sources of income is to broaden what you do for money, what you sell, and what services that you provide.

As an example, let's say that you are a printmaker, specializing in etchings, and for the last few years you have been creating abstracted images of cityscapes. What can you do to bring in some extra income, broaden your audience, and raise the perceived value of your original work? Since you work in multiples, you have something of an advantage over artists who create things one at a time, even if you limit your print runs.

There are other things that you, the printmaker, can do to grow your business as an artist, and to have multiple sources of income. Continue showing and selling your original work. To immediately raise the prices on this work, present your work in higher-quality and better-looking frames. Meanwhile, experiment with small, quick monotypes of your abstracted cityscapes and have them available for sale as well. Hold a few workshops demonstrating any special methods that you may have developed. Think about reproducing a few of your images on other products such as notecards or a set of slightly-abstracted-cityscape-urban-wear t-shirts.

You have an imagination, no question. Use that brilliant imagination of yours to come up with some great ideas (and a bunch of silly ones along the way for your own entertainment). With some thought applied to your situation, you will have a variety of ideas to create more inexpensive options to offer the people who love your work, no matter what condition their finances may be in.

The more ways that you grow your business as an artist, and the more you get out there, the more name recognition you will acquire. And the more that people recognize your name, as an artist, then the higher the perceived value of your original work will be.

Growth as an Artist

Constantly strive to improve the quality of your work. Learn new skills, push yourself to always do better, and try new approaches within your current body of work. If you paint from photographs, then try painting from life with all its magnificent challenges. Learn to draw.

You don't want to be all over the place, but with your own artistic sensibilities, your own vision and your own artist's hand, over time your work will naturally evolve. And by that process, improve. You will gain more interest and enthusiasm in what you do, which will show in your work. As you gain new skills, you will build more of a repertoire, and more of an audience. It's still all you.

Expand your sense of color, look sideways at your subject matter and play with materials and tools that are new-to-the-market and that have been developed for your medium. Reach into the deep files cloistered in the back recesses of your head. See what you have in there and bring something forward; an old idea that you meant to work with someday or a postponed interest in stark black and white, when all your life you have been working in rainbows of color.

Know that not every piece you create will be better than the one right before it. In any given year you will probably create some disappointing work, a few truly dull stubs, remarkable in their fifteen flickering watts of anti-brilliance. It's okay. We all come up with this stuff. The important thing is that in any given year as a whole, your work has improved and grown from the previous year, or at the very least, you have made your best effort to do so.

For a true artist, in my opinion, that perfect painting (or that perfect sculpture, drawing or tapestry), is always just outside our grasp. This is something we can only define for ourselves as individual artists. We improve a little bit each time as we seem to get closer, yet the more we know and understand about our medium of expression, the more our perfect vision nudges itself a little further beyond our reach. This is what we strive for as artists, and it's truly a magnificent process. It may sound annoying, but this is what keeps us going. If we actually got there, if we actually created the perfect painting (sculpture, drawing, tapestry), then what would we do with ourselves?

There is a difference between exploration and being lost when it comes to growing as an artist. One is purposeful, and the other is simply... lost.

Exploration is defined by going on any new path with all your senses keenly attuned to the possibilities. You may have the intention of finding something, with an open interpretation of what that something might be, whether it is inside or outside of yourself. When you are exploring you are purposeful, and also very open to what you might find along the way, even if you are chasing after an elusive vision.

It is possible to shift from lost to exploring, even during the process. For example, let's say that you work in clay, but have been curious about watercolor for a long time. You are good at what you do, but you feel somewhat stuck and need to clear your head a bit. You think that maybe trying a new medium which focuses on color, you might come up with some new ideas for glazing, while stepping outside the world of clay. Or maybe your kiln is broken, it won't be fixed for another two weeks, and you want something creative to do while you wait.

You buy a set of watercolors, a few brushes and some paper. You say to yourself "today I am going to just let go and see what happens". And off you go. Since you are already good at something you probably have high expectations of yourself. Now, as an oil painter, I will tell you that watercolor is a difficult medium to master. And here you have made a horrible mess (believe me, I have done the same with pastels). This is not a joyous mess, but a defeated mess. You feel frustrated, and not especially proud of yourself for trying something new.

To shift from this state to one of healthy exploration, look at watercolor paintings and find some that you admire. Talk to some watercolorists. Focus on following a technique. Or start exploring by mixing colors and making stripes. Don't worry about picture making just yet (which would be focusing on finding something vague). Combine a few guidelines with an open mind and minimal expectations. Play with a purpose. Growth will come from there.

Remember that creative setbacks are normal. We all have our bad days, which sometimes stretch into uninspired weeks. Ride them out, clean out your studio (which will also help to clean out your head), try something new, go look at other peoples' artwork, oh, and buy my book on creativity; 'Drawing Out the Muses' for countless other ideas.

Successful growth comes with the time that you commit to being serious about yourself as an artist. This is not just about how much time you commit each day or week, but to the time that accumulates over years when you dedicate your life to being an artist. The most important thing is that you give it your all, if being an artist is truly who you are. Yes, there will be times when family or health or economic issues take precedence. However, if your dedication to your life's work is solid, then your art can safely ride out these temporary setbacks when you are not in your studio, even if whole months are involved.

What you do when you are in your studio is the most important thing of all. The work you create and the process of creating it is what being an artist is all about. The career and the business end is primarily about supporting the creation of that art, and might also be about getting your ideas out there. Without the actual artistic process happening in sincerity, there is no real reason for the other stuff.

There truly is a market for anything and everything. You do not need to fit your work to match some imagined limited marketplace in any medium or handling of subject matter. If you create work that is truly from your heart, then soon enough someone will be touched enough by it to want to have it for their very own. Follow your own muse.

I have sold a wide cross-section of artwork over the years; photography, monotypes, etchings, beadwork, mixed-media on wood, acrylic on canvas, oil on canvas, oil on paper and oil on hardboard panel. I have even sold paintings on canvas board and scrap pieces of canvas. I have sold unfinished work. I have sold still-lifes, portraits and landscapes: realist, surrealist and abstract. I have sold allegorical work, beautiful, whimsical, serious and tragic work. I have sold 5 x 7 inch paintings and 4 x 6 foot paintings.

When I look back at what I have sold in all this time, the only pattern I can see is that there is no pattern. I cannot predict what any collector might want, so therefore I create exactly what I desire to create. This is a precious freedom, but one that also works according to my personal experiences in the marketplace. Many other artists will tell you the same thing, and you may have already seen this with your own experiences.

However, if you need to produce a guaranteed marketable body of work for steady income, then realize that it's just another day job, similar to doing commissioned work. You are creating artwork to someone else's specifications, even if they are suggested by past sales, or are recommended by your dealer and not an actual commission. This is not an art crime, but neither is it easily conducive to artistic growth. However, there are two things that you can do to stretch your own boundaries while creating similar work over and over again:

1. If you have a good income from such an artistic day job then consider yourself lucky on the financial security level, especially if this occupation supports your creative vision and growth. This means you must do your best to make time to create for yourself, to follow your own vision. You can separate the two. It is possible. Designate one easel or worktable or loom for the regular income-producing work, and another for your own creative work. Separate your workspaces and separate your

working time. Be very clear to yourself about which is day job time and when the hours are purely yours.

2. If you cannot afford the luxury of two workspaces (even in the same room), and time is crunchy as it is, then try to incorporate a challenge into each piece of artwork. Keep control over your backgrounds, try new color schemes or use line in a different way. Find new ways to approach the same old thing that somebody out there is expecting of you. Add a little bit of fun to the process. This way, something in the piece will be truly your own, and you will have had the chance to learn and grow while in the process of pleasing someone else.

Many of the great master artists of centuries past were court painters and/or did work commissioned by the church. The best of them found a way to do their own work as well. They can be your role models.

The Variable Factors

This chapter was originally called Intangibles, because all the factors discussed here cannot be mathematically quantified. However, the dictionary definition of the word intangible related to something that was way too vague. And these variable qualities can be measured or compared in one way or another. All of them will inform your pricing structure to some degree.

Every item discussed in this chapter needs to be balanced with the cold hard facts of your mathematical calculations. All of the things mentioned here will affect which price range your work falls into. No matter what the total cost of creating a piece of art, if the goods aren't there, your expenses won't matter much to the collector. You can spend 50 hours of time and $500 on materials and overhead, but if the finished piece is not that good, then all the effort and money spent will make no difference. It is who you are and what you put into your work that completes the picture.

I personally believe that the most important, no excuses variability is the quality of your work, followed immediately by originality and then the structural and/or archival integrity of the piece. Sometimes, it's all about fame or having a dealer that plays "emperor's new clothes" successfully.

In random order, the variable factors involved with pricing your artwork are:

1. The artist's technical ability as shown in the quality of the artwork
2. The artist's originality of vision; their creativity
3. The quality of the piece of artwork, and its archival structure
4. The background years spent developing technical ability and vision
5. Longevity and consistency in being an artist over the years

6. Career level as shown by the individual and collective items on the artist's resume
7. Education and credentials
8. Name recognition
9. Reputation
10. Comparison to other artists creating similar work in medium, size, ability and career level
11. The current art market and the price range limits of the market for similar work

The Economy and the Art Market

The economy should not affect your prices, although it may affect your sales to some degree. Even though lowering your prices is not a good idea as outlined in the chapter on Consistency, if the general economy is down, then it may not be a good year to raise them either. Hold your prices steady, let things begin to catch up, and make a few confident sales before raising them. Despite what some people are saying, artwork is being sold.

The long-term art market is not all that tied to the immediate economy. It is what you will observe over years of visiting galleries and paying attention to other artists' sales. You will eventually get a feel for it, with a good sense of where things are and where they should be.

The short-term art market can be tied to the current economy. There may be less or more money circulating at any given time, but like anything in flux, it eventually passes, it changes, it goes through its cycles. Maybe some gallery sales are down, but other venues might be doing well, such as artists' open studios or high-end craft shows. Artwork still gets bought and sold even during the slow periods. Neither the immediate economy nor the short-term art market should affect your pricing structure. However, when the economy does slow down, you will clearly see why it is good to have more than one thing going, and why it is important to have work available in different price ranges.

Price Ranges in the Art Market

An important factor in relating your pricing structure to the art market is the general price range for what you do. The current market for similar work sets the limits for reasonable pricing. This involves matching your prices (when first setting them) to what the market will bear. Ideally, the calculations end of your pricing structure will fall into this equation. If your costs fall within the limits of the range, then the other variables apply.

For example, unless an artist is advanced in their career, famous, and/or very accomplished, you can expect that the market will bear a price range of $500 to $4,000 for a small oil painting. Why such a wide scope in prices? This is where the other variables discussed in this chapter will come into play.

For example, if it costs a painter $1,500 to create a small oil painting, with a 50% commission factored in it could then retail for $3,000. Either way, the painting falls into the market range for small oil paintings by early to mid-career artists.

If you put in the hours and the overhead and you find that the cost of creating your work is over the comparable price range, then your work must be absolutely superb. The collector will also expect that expensive or rare materials were incorporated into the piece and/or that you used a very complex process in creating it. Otherwise, check your overhead costs. Are they miscalculated? For example, don't average in the rent on a studio that you barely use during the year.

How does one find this mysterious price range? It takes some time and research, as well as clearheaded observation. Go to exhibitions, go to galleries, go to art fairs, go to wherever artwork is for sale. Always keep an eye out for what similar artwork is selling for, especially when red dots are involved. The red dots will let you know that people are buying art at those particular prices, not just that artists are setting them. After awhile, you will get a good feel for what the selling price ranges are for work that is similar to yours in medium, size, quality, originality, etc.

Cumulative Experience

If an artist has spent many years developing their technical ability and original vision, then it must be worth something. In some ways, this experience is worth everything. No artist could make great, unique, well-crafted artwork if it were not for all those years in practice. The work would not be that accomplished.

For example, someone is interested in buying a piece of your art, but they want to know why it costs so much if you spent only 35 hours in time and support work creating it. Did you just sit down for the first time ever at the easel, wheel or press and spend 35 hours creating this piece? NO! You've spent years, maybe decades getting to this point, developing the skills to be able to create such high-quality works of original art. The time and effort spent becoming the artist you are now is a very important factor.

I am not aware of any mathematical formula for calculating experience. There could be a value applied per year, but it is not concrete as a mathematical value. How do you decide what each year is worth? How does one add the intangible value of all that experience? Maybe it is the X factor. Like some other things in this chapter, researching comparisons with other artists who do similar work will play an important role in calculating the semi-intangible.

Age is a virtue for artists, despite what we are sometimes told. The skill and wisdom gained through years of practice is considerably valuable. We are lucky this way. There is always a future. Youth is where many of us start on this journey, and some artists join us later along the trail, but the path always leads forward.

Being Objective About Your Artwork

How can you be objective about something as subjective as your own artwork? It's not too hard, but it takes self-discipline. The initial thing is to feel good about being an artist. The first step in comparing yourself to other artists is to not feel threatened by comparisons. The key thing to realize is that you are where you are at in your abilities and your career at this moment and you should applaud yourself for at least that much. So many people don't listen to their desires, follow their dreams, or have a relationship with their muses and you do. You have the courage and fortitude to be an artist. Countless others have given up along the way.

Okay. So far, so good. You venture out to an exhibition and you see work that you admire. Maybe this means that the artist has outstanding skill or they see things in a really interesting way that you never thought of before.

Maybe they are better at what they do than you are. By all means, please feel good about what you see. You are inspired. You have something new to aspire to. Don't become jealous. Chances are they worked really hard to get to that point. You can work that hard too, and produce amazing artwork that other artists will admire. They are a positive example for you.

I always felt that looking at others' artwork was a win-win situation. Seeing really good work is a treat. And when you see work that is not so great, then you can feel like you are not the worst artist ever. In fact, you can probably feel pretty good about your place in the scheme of things. Either way, it's a positive experience. So, go out and see a whole bunch of artwork, hundreds, thousands of pieces. This amount will add up pretty easily.

To learn to be objective you will have to look at a lot of art. You will also need to know your various techniques well and understand the basics of art history. Go to local shows, galleries, art centers and museums. When you travel, schedule time to look at art. It is especially helpful to see what artists in other states, and other countries, are doing. Look at mass amounts of art; all styles, genres, sizes, skill levels, even other mediums. Eventually, you will acquire a good sense of where you fit in at this time.

Do you have either an over-inflated ego or insufficient self-esteem? I'm no psychologist, but try to check your true feelings when observing others' work. What are your emotions doing in reaction to what you see? Do you become agitated, feel a little too self-important or do you sink into a temporary depression? This is how you feel when subjective emotions take control.

On an average day of gallery hopping, you will see possibly 30 to 40 different artists' works. How do you feel by late afternoon? At the end of the day if you feel okay, or even a little better than when you started, then you know you are clearheaded enough to be objective. Some of the art may excite or interest you, and some pieces will draw you in for a closer look. Other pieces bore you or you may feel indifferent. You're basically happy for the other artists and happy for yourself at the same time. None of what you see feels like a threat to your sense of self. You may be inspired enough to know where you need to improve and that's good. You are also able to see how you are doing just fine in your journey, that you're on the right path.

In order to be objective about the quality of a piece of artwork, and the technical skill of the artist that created it, you will need to know your own technique and materials well. You will need an intense knowledge of what you do, to the point where you can read how another artist created a piece just by looking at it carefully.

This does take time however, sometimes years of knowing your medium. You will need to know what place your medium and technique has in art history. You will need to see what hundreds of artists are doing, and have done, in your medium. Go to countless exhibits. Look through countless art books. The more time you spend doing and looking and learning, the more objectively and clearly you will be able to compare artwork.

To compare artwork similar to yours, you will need to look at everything you can in your medium. Examine all aspects of technique, style, materials, and not just the particular details of your thing, which might be realist miniature figure sculptures in bronze.

If you are such a sculptor, look at sculpture in all mediums from clay, metal, glass, wood and stone to mixed-media works, from carved to cast to fabricated sculpture, and in all sizes. Consider the thought behind both realist and abstract sculpture. Look at the work from all angles and examine the materials closely. Think about how the artist might have constructed such a thing. How would you do something similar with your knowledge of the medium, and in your own medium, if it is a different one?

What if you are a painter? There are two basic ways to approach a painting. One is to look at the picture, which is what most people have been taught to do. This is also our natural inclination. The other is to look at the actual painting. Start with looking at the picture, since paintings obviously involve the picture plane.

In looking at the picture you will notice the following things; color, composition, entrance (where your eye enters the picture plane), picture flow and breathing space. Is it representational, abstract or one of hundreds of shades in-between? Is something being portrayed, is there a story, an allegory, an emotional response, or is it a painting concerning itself only with art theory?

When you are looking at the technical aspects of the painting you will notice things such as the direction of the brushstrokes or knife work, individual colors, the quality of paint (thick, thin, opaque, transparent), and the depth of the surface. After a number of years of both looking at paintings, and of course actually creating paintings, you will be able to examine these things with ease.

As one more example, if you work with the more traditional fiber arts, then look at weavings, tapestries, soft sculpture, knotted work and quilts. You can also look at crochet, knitting and embroidery (you will see some cool stuff). Pay attention to the different types of yarn, and qualities of fabric and other fibers that were used in the piece. Notice color, pattern, functionality, pictorial elements and unique attributes. Maybe the artist added other materials such as buttons, beads, chicken bones, whatever their imagination told them to add. After looking at hundreds of pieces in a wide variety of fiber work, both traditional and experimental, from beginner to advanced professional, you will get a good idea of where you are in the grand scheme of things.

Checking Your Career Level

Comparing your career level to other artists is easy to do, but it takes some research as well. Look at your resume. How many items do you have listed on how many pages? When you go to galleries or open studio events, you will often find artist resumes available for all to see, sitting on a table or the front desk with the postcards and the show catalogs. Peruse them whenever you get the chance. You can also find resumes on many artist websites, although they may not be complete because of their length. The artist resume is also referred to as a curriculum vitae or CV.

Compare your resume with artists who do similar work with a comparable level of skill (or at least in the same medium). An artist with a few shows, two reviews, and only one award will command lower prices for their art than someone who does equal work, but whose resume has three full pages of items. A resume will also tell you for how long, and how consistently, an artist has been working, or at least how long they have been paying attention to their career. When looking at a resume, also notice the size of the print and the spacing. These devices are good for filling out the first page if the artist is just starting in their career, but they can be obviously deceptive for someone trying to fill a second page or more. Be honest with everything you have listed on your resume and don't make things up, which can come back to bite you later on.

It is not only the amount of items listed on the resume, but the quality of those items that is important. In my early years I had listed a number of café and restaurant exhibits, which are excellent opportunities for artists beginning their careers. However, by the time my resume was two pages full of small print, I decided to drop those listings because they weren't as impressive as showing in spaces dedicated solely to viewing art. When removing things from your resume, you can add the word "selected" to the category title, which is then accurate.

By seeing a large cross-section of other artists' resumes you will get a good feel for what yours should look like. The following items are the basic artist resume categories, followed by a few questions worth considering in reference to the details of the listing. Here they are, in no particular order:

1. Solo and group exhibition history – Where was the exhibit located? Was it in a café, an art center, a gallery or a museum?

2. Publications and reviews – Was the coverage local, regional or national? Was it a positive review or simply a mention of the artist's name in a long list of other artists? Was there an accompanying image of the artist's work?

3. Grants and awards – How prestigious was it, what time period was it for and how difficult was it to receive?

4. Lectures and presentations – How prestigious was the event, where was it held and to whom was it presented?

5. Private and public collections – How many, where and to whom?

6. Related experience – Is the artist a teacher, do they lead workshops, are there important commissions or anything else of interest as it relates to being an artist?

7. Education – Which schools, ateliers, workshops and/or residencies were attended? Were any degrees or certificates earned by the artist, and if so, which ones? Did they study independently or apprentice with an artist-teacher?

If you are just starting out as an artist, or if you are in the early stages of your career, it is still a good idea to look at the resumes of more accomplished artists. This research will help guide you on your path with your career. Make a point of seeking out showings of other relatively new artists. You will find their work on the walls of cafés, some alternative spaces, student exhibitions, membership galleries, annual community shows at art centers and at open studio events. The work of artists who are further along in their careers can also be seen in many of these places, giving you a nice cross-section to study.

Comparing Creativity Levels

While you are out there gallery hopping, looking at resumes and staring down technical skills, pay attention to the issue of creativity. Do you see mostly the same old repetitious themes, viewpoints and treatments to the same old subjects? Or are you seeing work that is different, unique, truly one solitary artist's take on things? After looking at scores of artwork you will clearly see that which is highly creative. Look at all the artwork in your medium with an eye focused on the various levels of creativity. After some time, you will be able to see how original your work is in comparison.

Now, if you are in love with painting flowers, or any other common theme, and have no plans to change course, that's fine. However, paint those flowers in your very own way. Portraying a traditional subject from a new viewpoint is much harder to do well than working with new subject matter. It is more of a challenge, and is not to be dismissed lightly. Distinctive work will help with your level of public recognition. More importantly, it is work expressed by your own personal vision of the world.

Reputation and Recognition

Recognition is simply name fame. Reputation is what stands behind that name. However, recognition is needed for an artist's reputation to become known. Both things will affect your price levels. Fame can breed money. Some collectors take comfort in buying a familiar name. Others will take their chances and purchase art which they genuinely prefer. The more name recognition you have equals the more opportunities you will have to sell artwork to both types of collectors.

Recognition comes with being active in the world. Being visible, both with yourself and with your work, and being active in your career will gain you recognition over time. Your reputation will grow from the quality and originality shown in your work. How you behave as a professional artist, and if your future looks promising, will also affect your reputation.

Educational Background

Somewhere along the way in the last century or so, the education of artists slipped out of the workshops and ateliers and joined the college and university system. Technique was replaced by theory. The degree, preferably an MFA, became a sign that one was a serious artist. By the 1990s two extremes concerning artists' education became the requirement for success in the art market, or at least they told us so; having a Master of Fine Arts degree or having absolutely no education at all. I have a BFA. Duh.

In my opinion, an education, no matter where one gets it or how it is achieved, is only a means by which an artist may learn something about creating art and is not a marker for which that art or artist should be judged. Any credentials are questionable because of how they may have been acquired. It is the abilities of the artist and the quality of their work that is the true measure of artistic achievement.

Value

I use the word "value" a lot in this book, whether it is in reference to valuing oneself as an artist or in considering the value of a piece of artwork. It is a word that can easily become overused to the point of distortion, not just here, but in many situations. I could quote from the dictionary, but instead I recommend that you look it up for yourself. There are so many meanings and interpretations. You wouldn't want to miss any of them.

Some random thoughts on the word "value" as it relates to artwork:

1. The value of something can mean its equivalence in money, or anything for which it may be bartered

2. There is intellectual value, wherein provenance and art history may play a role

3. There is emotional value, meaning there is some kind of personal attachment

4. It may be something that is not easily replaced due to rarity

5. And then, some old stuffed toy may be very valuable to you for whatever reason, but it might not fetch $3.00 at a yard sale

6. Individual perception is very much involved in the meaning of value

Valuing something means that you believe in it having worth. Value in the context of art, the actual, completed piece of artwork, implies high quality and craftsmanship. This comes with hard work over years of developing the skills and vision that collectively go into the time spent completing each piece. Valuable art is not cheap, but neither is it overpriced.

Why Art has Value

One of the main arguments against considering art valuable as anything other than an investment is that it is not useful. Considering that most investments are crapshoots these days, usefulness becomes a useless concept under these terms. However, if someone is investing in art to build a collection to enjoy, to share with others, to pass on to future generations, to create an endowment, etc., then it is a very useful investment.

The joke sometimes goes that art is only useful for such things as hiding stains, holes and cracks in the wall. Sculpture can used as a doorstop. Useful is an object that can be used, like a tool, and only useful things have real, tangible value.

So, how are useful things valued on the market? Who decides? On what terms are these useful items priced? Go into any variety store, big box store or the nearest mall and look around. Why are different nails, socks, toasters, notebooks, folding chairs, can openers and shampoo all priced the way they are? Why is there such a price range for any one given category of item? The raw materials involved are only a partial explanation.

And then, why do we spend money on music, books, education, entertainment, or spiritual retreats and so on if these things are not tangibly useful? Art is useful in similar ways to any of these things. If there is value only in that which is purely functional, then why do we paint walls different colors instead of leaving them sheetrock white and mud brown? Why aren't all plates colored clay gray and clothing only shades of raw cotton and wool beige? Why do we have pets and not just livestock? What about there being different colors and styles in cars, furniture, shoes, clothing and hairdos? Realize that usefulness and functionality can be defined in many different ways.

Visual artwork is extraordinarily useful on the following levels: spiritual, emotional, intellectual, inspirational, historical and decorative. People sometimes buy art to define themselves, whether it is to express their inner selves with art they admire or can relate to, or they are simply showing off their investments. Art can be an archival keepsake, a record of the times to be passed down through generations. Yes, it's quite possibly a luxury item. So are fresh organic blueberries and owning more than two pairs of shoes at any one time. Art can be an inexpensive luxury, and some well-appreciated luxury now and then is a very good thing. It's relative.

There are countless ways that art can be useful and therefore valuable to the collector, and any reason considered is valid. If so many people across time and distance have the natural impulse to create art, and so many more people desire to have it around, then the visual arts has tremendous value to humanity. Enough said.

Finding the Value in an Individual Piece of Art

There are various characteristics that give an individual piece of artwork value. These attributes are demonstrated in the work by beauty, timelessness, the artist's unique creative vision, technical excellence, intellectual and inspirational qualities, rarity, and archival construction. An artist's reputation and career history also adds to the value of a piece of art.

If you have been dedicated to your work for a long time and have a clear understanding of where your own artwork fits into both the contemporary scene and as a part of the continuing history of art, then you will see where the value in your work lies. Take every issue I have discussed in this book and add a few of your own to the mix. If you can step outside of yourself and be completely objective, then you can see the intrinsic value in each piece of art that you create. You will be able to decide for yourself the value of your work, and you will then be able to communicate that value to collectors, curators and anyone else. See the chapter called The Variable Factors for information on how to measure this.

The Value of Artists to Society

Human expression affects all our lives deeply. It is who we truly are as a culture, and the visual arts play a great role. Through our varied creativity, and with keen perception and observation, we enrich the society in which we live in countless ways. We are needed as a means to see things differently, and to present what we see ahead of the curve.

We document, we explore, we reflect, we interpret, and we comment on every facet of this complex world. We give much of ourselves, and our lives, in order to do so. And the truth is that most of us want to give, but we must also have the means to give in order to be able to do so.

The Value of Artists to the Economy

The arts provide tremendously to the economy. This has been well documented. Many studies have been made on the positive impact that the arts have on the general economy: locally, regionally and nationally.

If we are in business, then we support a multitude of other businesses in the process of being artists. We spend money on supplies, tools, equipment, studio furniture, lighting, packaging, etc. We utilize the services of framers, printers, photographers, web developers, shipping services, and many others. Everything that is on your material and overhead expenses list, everything you spend money on as an artist, benefits another business, which then has more money to circulate into the economy. As working citizens we also spend money on the basic necessities of life. If we are doing well, then we have some extra money to spend. Money circulates. The more money that is circulating, the healthier the economy is. Plus, artists are taxpayers too. Artists add to the economy, we add to the quality of life for everybody and we are vital to the culture. Period.

We also raise the value of real estate, whether we like it or not. Look at what artists have done for neglected downtowns and abandoned warehouse districts all over the country. The things we do for real estate, however unintentionally, should earn us major commissions as a group. Artists are the impetus for revitalizing many industrial urban areas. Then, when it's deemed safe, all kinds of other economies follow us, such as clubs, restaurants, trendy shops, loft condominiums, etc., to the point where many of us can't afford the kind of space we need anymore. And so we migrate somewhere else and the cycle starts all over again. Everyone wants to be where the artists are, living in lofts and storefronts and carriage houses, and oops, where have all the artists disappeared to now?

Confidence

Being an artist is not a hobby, but a vocation. It is a calling that we must respond to. I say this a lot, but it's true. We have an inherent need to visually interpret the world around us by using our hands, minds and certain materials to create art. I often say that the only choice I have in the matter is to choose to follow this calling or to deny my authentic being the only thing it really wants. Does the world owe us a living because of this? No. But if someone wants to buy the fruits of our labor (and our passion), then these costs must be considered in the price of our work.

Think about everything you have ever done to get to where you are today. What you have sacrificed in time, finances, relationships, housing, leisure, health and/or sufficient sleep? Too much time spent away from our studio, from working on our art, brings us pain and frustration. The need to create is that powerful.

The stereotype of the starving artist, while harmful in my opinion, has been rendered somewhat moot over the past decade. There is no job security anymore, no matter the profession. You may as well do what you love, even if you can only do it on a part-time basis. The fewer regrets you have towards the end of your life, the better.

This can be a tough profession, but it's worth it. There will be setbacks. But for every disappointment, give yourself a day or three to feel sorry for yourself, if you need to, and then move forward. Lick your wounds, then pick yourself up, dust off your knees, and put one foot in front of the other. Move forward.

If you feel as though you've paid more than your share of dues, then great. You're all paid up. You have more than earned any measure of success you receive from here on in.

Gratitude

There are countless benefits to being an artist. We are often around other interesting people. We live surrounded by artwork. The world is much more fascinating for us, since we are aware of visual and tactile things that elude many other people. We can also see the stories in the many scenes of life. We have a keen observation and a natural means of expressing ourselves. We have a purpose in life. This is an enormous gift we have been given.

When you are going through a tough time, list everything that you're thankful for: the use of your eyes, your hands, your mind, your unique abilities and finely tuned sensibilities. Deckled paper, a new tube of cadmium red deep oil paint, that perfect chisel, a soft skein of cerulean blue lambswool, a block of white stoneware clay. The beautiful food waiting in your kitchen at the end of the day. A purring cat, a wagging dog, and the way the setting sunlight reflects off of a brilliantly glowing wall. Keep going. The world is full of simple and wonderful gifts. You will begin to feel pretty rich after a short while.

Be grateful that you're an artist. It's a royal pain sometimes, but would you really want to be anybody besides who you are? We are so fortunate that we have this means of creative expression, this way to deeply touch others. And it is fine, realistic, even idealistic, to be both grateful for the good things in your life, and at the same time, to want to correct what is not so good, to fix whatever needs improving. In fact, this is the best way to live. It's called being in balance.

Community

How do we fix the things that relate to the arts that need changing? Begin with yourself. Reclaim your own power by gaining knowledge of all the things that affect you as an artist. Raise your standards, both artistically and professionally. Raise the standards of how you act towards others and how you expect to be treated.

We should be sharing information with each other. Too many artists give in to fears about competition. However, we can look out for our own interests first, without being exclusive. There are some things you might need to keep private and that's okay. Just the same, we would all do well to share information with each other, especially about how the art world runs, what experiences we've had and how things might be changed for the better. Keeping our individual knowledge and experience from each other is a waste of collective intelligence and resources. Being non-competitive and sharing information benefits all of us. The more generous you are with what you know, the more will eventually be given back in return.

Don't quit. The broader culture needs you. The more diversity of vision there is, the richer we all become. Remember, it is better to be a part-time artist than to not be an artist at all. And some part-time artists do eventually get to be full-time artists; through hard work, sheer will, and with a little luck. Seize every possible opportunity that makes sense to you. There are folks in power in the art world who do deserve to be there and who take their responsibilities seriously. Some of them are really nice people too. They are worth meeting, so get out there.

Communicate with other artists. Seek out kindred spirits. Discuss the state of things. Build bridges with independent musicians, writers, actors, dancers and others. Develop a community of vibrant creative people. We are at a crossroads. Communication is the key. Community is the door to the best of all worlds.

An Addendum for These Times

Things are different now. Most of us didn't see it coming, not quite like this. The ups and downs, and then the further downs we thought were left behind in the gilded age. The rolling waves of economic flux mostly heave upwards for just a few. What remains of the secure middle class only has so much wall space. And it's usually the middle class who buys the art that living artists sell.

What do we do in an economy treated as a zero-sum-game? If things were flowing, if money were circulating throughout the economy, as it should, then it would be working for all of us. If the economy worked for most people once upon a time, then it could again.

Artists are not immune to politics. Pay attention.

So, what do we do? Besides, of course, lending our talents and creativity to causes of change and the betterment of society. Besides supporting the few political candidates not owned by corporations. Besides not giving up on either the country at large or our own personal careers.

Fewer works sell than before and more works pile up in spaces demanding ever-increasing rents. What to do? When you have to eat, or pay down student loans, or pay off stacks of bills... or in my case, wish to move forward in life and need some serious seed money in which to grow new trees (of opportunity)... what can we do?

This is how I am handling the situation:

I've been painting for a long time, which means I have a lot of work available. My prices have always been very reasonable for the quality of work that I do. I know what my paintings have sold for in the past, and what they are still selling for. My newest body of work, the one I am developing now, the variously abstract landscapes; each painting takes less time to create than the previous two bodies of work did per painting on average, and I can therefore charge less per piece; nearly half for a comparably-sized painting, while still covering my basic costs. This is a happy accident. I am painting what I paint according to my demanding muse and nothing else.

Some of this new work is top-notch, and some of it still shows growing pains. But people like what they like, and they often fall in love with paintings that are not my favorites. Lucky for them. If it's not an exhibiting-quality painting, in my opinion and with my discerning eyes, then they can get it for less. I can price it lower because it needs to go. Maybe these pieces are the "factory seconds". This work is as archival as can be, there are no structural deficiencies, nothing is irregular or defective about any of these paintings, but I will just never put them on exhibit (in physical space), no matter what.

I have a number of paintings, some newer, some older, which are now being priced lower than my exhibition-quality work. These are mostly studies, practice pieces and experimental work. I want them to have homes, to be loved, to move on for themselves... and I could always use the money. These are paintings I will sell online. When the day comes I have an open studio situation again, I will sell them there as well.

Everything else from my current, and two previous, bodies of work are staying at their set prices for now. This is my accomplished work, the successful pieces, the better paintings, much of what I do. These prices will be raised at some point in the near future.

This is how some of my artist friends are handling things:

At the very least, their prices are staying static and/or relative and/or raised slightly on their best work, the exhibition-worthy work, the really good artwork. Newer, "cheaper" work is created and offered for sale, often on social media. I have seen dozens of $100. plein air sketches and figure sketches; small things, around 8 inches or so in either dimension, offered for sale. This is what I am seeing – quick and sweet little things offered at a very low price for original artwork. But that's fine. Groceries get bought this way. Other people collect art this way. Something good is happening and nobody is being exploited.

I will probably always say that you should not lower the prices on your best work. Don't lose money unless there is another pay-off, such as a career boost of some kind. Of course, I have the luxury to say this. I'm not going hungry. However, there are countless artists out there who are down to their last pocket of crumpled dollar bills. Do what you have to do to eat, stay housed, keep healthy. Call it a temporary sale, if you must. Keep your dignity and keep your belly full.

Things are different now. May they someday find their equilibrium again, preferably sooner than later.

More Books by Alexandria Levin

Drawing Out the Muses
Find and develop unlimited creative inspiration from the everyday world

Coming soon:
Pulling Abstraction from Realism

More titles are being developed for 2015
in both print and ebook formats.

Go to www.paintedjay.com for information and updates
on book availability and other news.

Connection Portal

Painted Jay Publishing
www.paintedjay.com

Alexandria Levin – oil paintings
www.alexalev.com

Alexandria Levin – graphic design, web development, lyric poetry and accidental photography
www.alexandrialevin.com

Bright Pink Smile – art blog
www.brightpinksmile.com

Made in the USA
Middletown, DE
16 August 2018